PUSH YOUR LIMITS

7 Secrets to Success

Unlock Your Potential: A Journey through Science and Spirituality to Achieve Your Goals

Ardy Constance

ISBN: 979-12-210-6917-4 (Paperback)
ISBN: 979-12-210-7764-3 (Hardcover)

TABLE OF CONTENTS

MY ACKNOWLEDGMENTS

To Romy, who tends to her family with great love, ceaseless devotion, and unwavering passion.

To my son who reminds me of how life is full of purpose and wonderful experiences.

To the angel that connects with me daily and brings me light and energy from the universe.

I would also like to thank Alessandra Veronesi at holyshiver.com for her friendship, counsel, and spiritual guidance.

I extend my heartfelt gratitude to all who have contributed to the creation of this book.

INTRODUCTION

Why did I call this book *Push Your Limits*? As I mentioned in the subtitle, it's about the 7 Secrets to Success. The secrets of pushing your limits to realize your vision of life are now yours to read. But how this book came to be is a story from my own life.

I realized at a very early stage of my youth that I had to learn the facts of life the hard way. My path was never easy, but I continued to pursue success despite those hardships.

My difficulties didn't stop me from sorting out the challenges I faced. I made a promise to myself: Never to give up on being who I was, being respectful of others, and maintaining an open mind about what life could give me every day. That meant taking both what's good and what's bad and making the best of it. I resolved to be humble and accept mistakes. I would listen to myself. I wouldn't be shy about asking for help, and I would persevere in my beliefs.

Those resolutions have served me well. I have been able to build a life for myself that's full of success. And now I'm here to share the secrets of that success with you. You, too, can believe in yourself and accomplish whatever you define as success. It could be a rewarding career, a loving family, deep relationships with friends and loved ones, or a legacy of wisdom to leave your descendants. Whatever your vision of success is, my purpose is to help you explore your own consciousness and stimulate awareness on ways you can push and pull your potential, thanks to the *7 Secrets of*

Success that I'll share with you in this book. Here's a brief look at what you'll discover:

You'll learn about how your brain and body are wired to give you the motivation you need to pursue your dreams. I'll help you understand the patterns that guide your life and how you can develop better habits that will improve how you approach life. Then, I'll help you dig deep into your beliefs about life and the world. I'll even show you ways to transform your beliefs so that they're more likely to lead you to the outcomes you desire.

After that, I'll share with you ways to find your higher purpose in life and the guiding principles that define how you will put your principles into action. Setting goals is an important part of the process, and I'll guide you through it. I'll show you how to build the confidence to pursue your goals and the resilience to respond to the challenges you'll face along the way. Loving yourself is one of the strongest powers you can have, and I'll help you build and nourish it. Taking care of your body and mind will also prepare you to accomplish your dreams. The secrets of self-care will build up your abilities and prepare you to persevere.

I can also help you explore your relationship to the universe! The wonders you'll find throughout the universe will astound you with their beauty and power. Most of all, your connections to the universe will allow you to recognize your own potential for greatness and prepare your spirit to achieve it. You'll learn to look within yourself and discover ways to manifest what you need and want most.

Along the path to fulfillment, there are moments when you will have to rethink and reprogram your lifestyle, let go, and pursue your goals without second thoughts. It will require shifting the conventional rules of reality and opening yourself to trusting the universal laws of manifestation. You must nurture positivity and happiness if your ambition is to succeed in what you do.

The universe is waiting to guide you. Your exploration of the wonders of creation, including yourself and the vast power of your brain, will help you find your way through the complexities of life. Together, they will provide you with a path you can follow to your vision of success.

Push Your Limits! is the ultimate guide to awareness and consciousness. It reveals the secrets that have always been waiting in your life for you to grasp. Just don't let anyone stop you from believing!

Chapter 1
THE SCIENCE OF THE BRAIN

Our minds influence the key activity of the brain, which then influences everything; perception, cognition, thoughts and feelings, personal relationships; they're all a projection of you.
– Deepak Chopra

Your brain is the most powerful computer in the world. It can store information, connect that information, regulate breathing, control speech, enable motion, and coordinate other vital functions. While all animals have brains, the human brain is extremely complex and effective at controlling your body and even your perceptions, reactions, thoughts, emotions, and memories. Without the power of the brain, human beings wouldn't be the intelligent, insightful, and awesome creatures that we are.

Your Brain's Wiring

The brain is made up of cells called neurons and connections called synapses. There are around 86 billion neurons in the human brain, and each one of those neurons can have as many as hundreds of thousands of synapses (Caire et al., 2023). That's a lot of brainpower!

The brain cells, called neurons, have structures called axons that extend from them. There are small gaps between the axons—the synapses I mentioned. The synapses convey messages between the neurons and to all parts of your body using a complex system of electrical and chemical (electrochemical) signals. The brain uses these signals to control all the parts of your body. They cause muscle fibers to fire, making them move. They signal your glands to release hormones that affect your internal organs and their functioning. And, perhaps most impressively, the neurons and synapses in your brain allow you to form and store memories, reason, feel emotions, react to the outside world, and even understand itself.

Your brain also allows you to interact with the world. You can see, hear, smell, taste, and touch the world around you. When your brain receives these sensations, it can identify and react to them. For example, your brain interprets what you see as a larch tree or a daisy. You can identify a sound as a guitar or a bird's song. It senses whether a smell is fragrant and pleasant or annoying and disgusting. Something you eat can taste sweet, sour, creamy, or crunchy. A piece of fabric can feel rough or smooth. Your perceptions help you make sense of the world.

Thought is perhaps the most impressive of all the brain's functions. How it translates those electrochemical reactions into thoughts about poetry, science, or philosophy is a mystery. How your brain creates and stores memories is better understood. Your body takes in information from your senses and translates it into electrochemical signals that are transferred by the synapses to the brain. When the brain gets overloaded with information, it can create new neurons and new synapses, so it doesn't run out of capacity.

The pathways that this information creates between the synapses in the neurons are essential to memory. The more a pathway is stimulated, the stronger the connection becomes, and the longer it's stored in memory. You have short-term memories that don't use the synapses very often, and these are memories you don't remember for very long. On the other hand, if you need to access a memory often, the stronger the connections are and the longer you remember it. For example, you might see a person you work with every day, so it's not difficult to remember their name. If you meet someone else one time at a party, their name is more likely to escape your memory the next time you see them.

Memory expert Paul Nowak (2023) explains that different kinds of memories are stored in different areas of the brain. For example, sights and sounds are stored in an area called the sensory cortex. Memories and information are stored in a separate area called the hippocampus. If your brain stores information in an organized way, it's easier to remember.

Nature and Nurture

But how does the human brain develop? For a long time, there were two major theories: nature and nurture.

According to the nature theory, genetics controls how the brain grows and changes. The qualities we inherit through our genes control how the brain develops and controls behavior. This was the dominant theory for a long time. What you were at birth determined what you would be like as you grew older.

The nurture theory, on the other hand, says that the environment you grow up in determines how you learn and what qualities you'll have. Your early experiences will control your brain development and, therefore, how you react to the world.

Modern brain scientists, however, believe that brain development is a combination of both nature and nurture. Neither one controls everything. They work together to create your personality and your behavior. Joan Stiles (2011) put it this way: "Brains do not develop normally in the absence of critical genetic signaling, and they do not develop normally in the absence of essential environmental input." She adds, "The fundamental facts about brain development should be of critical importance to neuropsychologists trying to understand the relationship between the brain and behavioral development."

What that means is that your genes create the wiring of your brain—the neurons and synapses that are responsible for the brain's functioning. The brain is programmed to have the ability to learn and grow in predictable ways. In the first months of life, a baby's brain is making new connections, creating the synapses that will send messages throughout the brain and body. That's all determined by nature.

What you learn is dependent on the environment you grow up in— your caregivers and how they nurture you. Your level of nutrition determines whether the body you're born with will grow strong. The love and care you receive will make it likely that you will grow up feeling secure and happy. The intellectual stimulation you're exposed to will help your natural intelligence develop and learn. That's the nurture part of the equation.

Your genetic heritage includes the ability to learn language, something that every baby is born with. However, the genetic aspect of the brain doesn't determine what language the child will speak. That comes from the environment they grow up in, listening to other people use language and learning to associate certain sounds with words, objects, and ideas.

Your personality is likely a combination of both nature and nurture. A baby can have a fussy temperament from birth, for example, but later learn how to deal with frustration by living with people who interact with them in a positive manner. If the caregivers aren't supportive and loving, however, this causes stress on the child, which may lead to behavior problems in the future. A baby with a sunnier disposition, smiles at caregivers who smile, laugh, and give other positive feedback to the baby, who learns to associate their faces with good feelings.

The Body's Wiring

The brain communicates with the rest of the body using the nerves to transmit messages. Nerves are often compared to wires that channel electrical messages throughout the body. Really, they are bundles of fibers that are wrapped into cord-like structures. The nerves convey signals from the brain to the muscles and organs of the body, telling them what to do.

An electrochemical message is created in the brain that tells muscles to contract, for instance. The message is transmitted through the nerves to the right muscles and causes them to contract or relax. If the messages go to the muscles in the hand and tell them to contract, for example, you make a fist.

The brain controls the human body through the nerves. The signals that travel up and down the nerves have a variety of effects. Besides causing muscles to contract and relax, the nerves send signals to the stomach and intestines to process food, to the fingertips to process sensations of touch, and to the adrenal glands to release a chemical that affects the heartbeat and respiration. They're grouped into motor nerves that cause movement, sensory nerves that relay sensations, and mixed nerves that serve both functions.

Nerves are connected from the brain to the body by the spinal column, or spinal cord. This is a long channel protected by bones that contains the most important nerves. Nerves branch off from the spinal cord to reach the sites where they act. For example, the nerves that control the legs and feet branch off the spinal cord near the base of the spine.

Nerves are also grouped into the sympathetic and parasympathetic nervous systems. They have complementary roles. The sympathetic nervous system carries messages from the brain that alert your body systems to danger or the need to be alert. The parasympathetic nerves send signals in the other direction in order to return the bodily systems to their normal functioning. The parasympathetic and sympathetic nervous systems carry out their functions without conscious control. You don't have to think about keeping your heart beating or your stomach digesting food.

The Brain-Body Connection

It's a fact that the brain is part of the human body. It's made up of cells like the rest of the body. The cells may differ in shape and function, but basically, they're the same at the most basic level of the structures within them and how they connect to each other. The body and the brain are two parts of one grand system. They are interconnected by the messages that are transmitted both electrically and chemically. The substances that do this are called, logically enough, neurotransmitters.

There are seven basic neurotransmitters that affect the brain and the body: glutamate, GABA, dopamine, adrenaline, serotonin, oxytocin, and acetylcholine. They all affect the brain and the body in different ways. Glutamate is the main substance that crosses the gap between neurons and synapses, transmitting messages not only within the brain but also within the body. GABA calms the brain. One of its functions is to help you sleep. Dopamine is intimately involved in your brain's system of rewards, which affects the formation of habits, which I'll get into in Chapter 2. Adrenaline controls how you respond to threats. It's produced by the adrenal glands but works throughout the body. Serotonin is a neurotransmitter that sends messages to your intestines as well as acting in the brain to influence your mood. Oxytocin is often called the "feel-good" or bonding chemical. It affects many body systems, including those that help you experience feelings of love and trust. And acetylcholine works where the nerves meet the muscles and affects both voluntary and involuntary movements.

That's not all there is to the mind-body connection, though. Recent research indicates that "parts of the brain area that control movement are plugged into networks involved in thinking and planning, and in control of involuntary bodily functions such as blood pressure and heartbeat" (Bhandari, 2023). Why does this matter? It may explain why people who have anxiety feel the need to pace. It may have something to do with why deep breathing helps calm the mind, mindfulness helps calm the body, and exercise improves your mood.

The Vagus Nerve

The vagus or vagal nerves are an important part of your parasympathetic nervous system. They run from your brain stem to your gut and have effects on the chest, heart, and lungs along the way to your digestive organs. It's the longest of the nerves in your body.

If the sympathetic nerves control reactions when the brain is excited and takes action, the parasympathetic nervous system serves to calm the brain and body back down. You don't have conscious control over this action. It happens without having to think about it. For example, you can't control your digestion, your immune system, or your heartbeat (unless you use special techniques such as meditation to slow the heart).

But the vagus nerve does other things as well. Bodily processes as varied as mood, saliva and urine production, speech, and taste are all affected by the action of the vagus nerve. Damage to the vagus nerve because of diabetes, viruses, and other causes can keep food from moving to the intestines. The vagal nerve can also cause you to faint if it overreacts to stimuli like extreme heat, anxiety, pain, or stress (Cleveland Clinic, 2022a).

It's also been found that, as "a critical component of the nervous system... the vagus nerve may help promote and protect brain function." Researchers say that "the vagus nerve also puts the brakes on inflammation, a key player in the onset of nearly all chronic diseases, including those that affect cognition" (Paturel, 2024). Devices that electrically stimulate the vagus nerve have been approved by the Food and Drug Administration to treat depression, migraines, and other conditions. Stimulating the vagus nerve may also be beneficial for the brains of healthy people.

Because the vagus nerve has a calming effect on the body and mind, it should not be a surprise that scientists are studying its connection to mental health conditions. In particular, "two neuroscience researchers at The University of Texas at Dallas are investigating whether vagus nerve stimulation (VNS) can accelerate recovery from emotional trauma in tandem with the most common type of therapy for patients." According to the scientists, "The goal is to shorten the duration and improve outcomes of exposure-based therapy, which is often effective but can be difficult for the patient" (Fontenot, 2022). In particular, VNS is being investigated for the treatment of traumatic memories, such as those that result from post-traumatic stress disorder.

You can protect your vagus nerve with a proper diet, exercise, and treatment of conditions like high blood pressure and diabetes.

Techniques including yoga, hypnotherapy, and meditation can also improve the functioning of the vagal nerves. Other techniques, such as massage, ice baths, and electronic vagal nerve stimulation, are also being investigated.

Responses to Stimuli

The brain has a great ability to respond to stimuli. When the senses encounter a stimulus, neurons send the message through the spinal cord to the brain. For example, the circuits that control movement react when the doctor hits your knee with a hammer. The brain sends a signal that causes your hand to flinch away when you touch a hot match. But physical sensations are not the only stimuli that the brain responds to. Words have an effect on the brain, too. They stimulate the brain to understand what the words refer to. They can also create other reactions in the brain. Many of these happen without any conscious control.

Fight, Flight, and Other Reactions

The nerves of the sympathetic nervous system control what is often called the fight-or-flight response. This response developed early in human history when large predators were a very real threat. In those circumstances, the best reaction to a threat was either to fight the attacking animal or run away from it.

The body responded to the threat with a flood of hormones that facilitated those responses. They're called stress hormones. Adrenaline is one of the most powerful. The stress hormones cause the body to respond in ways that make you fight or flee. The heart beats faster, blood pressure rises, breathing routes oxygen to where it's needed, and blood flows to the muscles. Attention and focus become keener as they concentrate on the threat. The fight-or-flight response increases the chance of survival.

Nowadays, except for very rare occasions, people aren't threatened by predatory animals very often. The occasional pit bull might attack you. When that happens, the body responds with the fight-or-flight response. Again, you get the hormonal boost that prompts you to run away from the dog. Fighting such a threat is less common, but there are cases when someone has fought off a cougar, an alligator, or a shark.

Unfortunately, there are other kinds of threats that you deal with in modern life. You can feel threatened by situations that cause you stress and anxiety, such as job interviews and public speaking. The nerves of the sympathetic system still operate as if there were a physical threat. You may feel faint or turn pale because blood flows to the muscles and away from the skin. Your hands shake because adrenaline floods your system. Even psychological threats can cause a fight-or-flight response.

Because all these responses come from the sympathetic nervous system, they happen without conscious thought. You don't have control over them, and you're not aware of that. That's why you're reacting so strongly. If you experience the fight-or-flight response often enough, you can fall prey to chronic anxiety and stress, even to the point of developing a psychological disorder. Your body will also suffer the effects, which can lead to cardiovascular and other physical problems.

But fight-or-flight isn't the only reaction possible to psychological threats such as abusive behavior like gaslighting. The two other possibilities are called freeze or fawn. Freezing isn't a response that would have helped in the case of an attacking predator, unless you thought that if you didn't move, the animal wouldn't notice you. But in the case of a psychological threat, freezing means that you aren't able to respond at all. You don't protect yourself by pushing back against an accusation, for example, or by fighting back if your partner attacks you physically.

The freezing reaction isn't beneficial, like the fight-or-flight effect. If you're being physically abused, freezing doesn't protect you from the attack. If you're being emotionally abused, freezing can anger your attacker and make them likely to continue the verbal attack.

The fawning response doesn't really work against psychological threats, either. If you have this reaction, you try to please the person by giving in to them or flattering them. If the psychological pressure goes on long enough, you act like a doormat.

Another drawback to the freeze and fawn reactions is that they don't prevent the stress hormones from affecting you physically. After this kind of interaction, you may find yourself shaking, panting, or turning pale. Your heart may race. And if it goes on too long, you can also experience the physical and psychological consequences of stress. Freezing or fawning doesn't get you away from the threat, so it can easily continue. And because, like fight or flight, these reactions travel along the sympathetic nervous system, you probably aren't aware of what's causing them.

Thoughts, Emotions, and the Brain

Two of the most important functions of the brain, besides controlling the body, are thoughts and emotions. The brain, despite being a physical organ, creates thoughts and emotions through the chemical signals of neurotransmitters. And your thoughts and emotions also have effects on your body and brain. Let's look at how it all works.

The Influence of Thoughts

When you think about the brain, you usually consider its power of thought. (Incidentally, thinking about thinking is technically called "metacognition". That's what we'll be doing here). There are different philosophies about what thoughts actually are. Does the brain itself, the actual organ, create thoughts? Or is the mind something separate from the brain, and does the mind create thoughts? Philosophers and neuroscientists have differing opinions, and the jury is still out. But here's the current point of view:

Thought is powerful. Your brain creates your thoughts, but the effects go both ways: Your thoughts also alter your brain chemistry. This changes not only physical structures in your brain but also in your body (Vilhauer, 2024). The neurotransmitters that control your body's interactions with the brain also control how your thoughts affect your body.

I've already discussed how experiencing stressful situations causes reactions that release neurotransmitters. Those neurotransmitters, in turn, influence your behavior, such as your fight-or-flight responses. But just thinking about stress can release those neurotransmitters as well. That's why even thinking about meeting your future in-laws for the first time can make your palms sweat before you ever see them. And thoughts can release neurotransmitters that cause you to use your muscles. For example, your thoughts cause you to reach for something you've dropped. It may feel automatic, but without the brain thinking, "That's falling," you wouldn't try to catch it. The thought starts the chain reaction.

You're creating thoughts now, just by reading this book. You may think that the explanations in it make sense. You might think that you want to read more about the brain. You might even think that you want to put the book down and take a nap. These thoughts trigger actions such as recommending this book to a friend, asking them to recommend another book, or going to bed.

Thoughts can pop into your head spontaneously when you're thinking about something else. Suppose you're reading a textbook or listening to a lecture, and you find yourself thinking about a vacation you have planned. That's caused by something called the "default mode network." It pulls up thoughts such as daydreaming, thinking of memories, or imagining the future. It happens when you're relaxed or bored rather than when you're focused on something important. You may feel that you're not in control of your thoughts, and to some extent, that's true. But you have the ability to change what you're thinking of and pay attention to the book or the lecture, for example.

Of course, your spontaneous thoughts aren't always good ones. You can also have intrusive memories or thoughts of unpleasant events that pop into your head at the worst possible time. If they're really serious and persistent, they can be flashbacks like the ones involved in post-traumatic stress disorder, obsessive-compulsive disorder, or another mental illness.

Your mental health is partially determined by your brain chemistry. If that chemistry is unbalanced, you can develop disorders such as bipolar disorder, generalized anxiety disorder, major depressive disorder, or schizophrenia. Of course, since we're talking about the brain, it's more complicated than that. Genetics and nurturing, as well as your experiences, can affect your brain and neurotransmitters.

The Influence of Emotions

Thoughts aren't the only things that emerge from the brain, however. The brain is the source of your emotions, too. Emotions come from a part of the brain called the limbic system, which is made up of several different structures. The hypothalamus, amygdala, and limbic cortex are all parts or regions of your brain that control your emotions. The hypothalamus controls emotions such as love and has other functions as well. The amygdala deals with responses to your environment, particularly fear and anger. And the limbic cortex affects happiness, mood, and motivation, which I'll talk about shortly. Damage to any of these parts of the brain can change how you respond emotionally to stimuli. Imaging studies indicate that brain networks are involved in emotions in addition to specific brain regions (Shackman & Wager, 2018).

Scientists disagree about how many different emotions there are. Six emotions—anger, fear, surprise, disgust, joy, and sadness—are considered common to all cultures, though other people say there are from 4 to 27 different emotions. Scientists also don't agree on whether these basic emotions are there from birth or develop through experience (Halber, 2018).

Much of your everyday life is governed by emotions. You desire and pursue the things that give you happy feelings and avoid things that cause you fear or disgust. Emotions can show on your face or be felt internally (your "gut reaction"). They can be expressed openly, but there are times when you must suppress your emotions, such as when someone angers you but you have to remain calm, or you have to suppress your desire to laugh at a solemn occasion like a funeral.

Another way that your emotions affect your body is how they influence your physical and mental health. Your immune system is sensitive to the effects of emotions, which can contribute to illnesses like colds or the flu, especially if you're emotionally stressed. Poor emotional health can also result in dry mouth, an upset stomach, and even sexual dysfunction. Then there are a number of mental conditions called mood disorders that are intimately involved with your emotions. If you have generalized anxiety disorder or major depressive disorder, you may need to get psychological help.

Many aspects of how the brain and body interact to create emotions are still unknown. It's difficult (and often unethical) to do experiments on human beings, and animal studies aren't adequate to reveal all the details. But it seems clear that human emotions can be at least partly controlled through techniques such as mindfulness and meditation.

Even good posture can make you feel more confident, and simply smiling can make you feel happier.

The Brain and Motivation

Motivation is what gets you up in the morning and what keeps you going, especially when you're working. Motivation is a vital force that revs you up and makes it possible to accomplish your goals and overcome setbacks. It's a necessary phenomenon for you to keep going and achieve. Without motivation, you drift through life at the mercy of outside forces. Let's take a look at what motivation is and how it operates.

What Is Motivation?

Some people think money is the best—or even the only—motivator. Others say that the best way to get motivated is to have a boss looking over your shoulder. Still, others say that you motivate yourself. They're all right, and they're all wrong. Those are examples of different kinds of motivation.

There are two different kinds of motivation: intrinsic and extrinsic. Intrinsic motivation comes from within you, while extrinsic motivation comes from something outside you. For example, you may have intrinsic motivation to practice playing the guitar because you enjoy it. It makes you feel good, so you're willing to work at it. Extrinsic motivation can come when someone tells you they like your guitar playing or when you get a paying gig. Extrinsic motivation comes when you think you'll receive a reward or avoid something unpleasant, like a bad review from your boss. Some people are more motivated by the prospect of getting a reward, while other people are motivated if they want to avoid a bad consequence.

Motivation can also help determine whether a reward is a want or a need and what you're willing to do to get it. If you intensely want a reward, such as a good job, you're more likely to work harder to get it than if the reward is just a trophy. The same is true with a need. If you have a basic need like good health, you're motivated to put more effort into getting it.

One aspect of motivation that gets a lot of attention is the risk-reward ratio. This refers to how much you're willing to risk bad outcomes weighed against the possibility of receiving a better reward. You often hear about the risk-reward ratio when investing money. Some people are willing to invest in riskier ventures if they think there will be a big payout. Others are more cautious, not willing to risk losing their money, and preferring a smaller but steadier return. Your emotional state may affect what you're willing to risk, and scientists are exploring that.

The Science of Motivation

How is the brain involved in motivation?

Connecting brain activity with motivation may seem like a simple matter, but it really takes a close look at neuroscience to explain the process.

Both intrinsic and extrinsic motivation are based on the reward system in your brain, which is controlled by a chemical called dopamine. Dopamine is one of the ways that your neurons communicate with other neurons. It works on areas of the brain that deal with emotions as well as planning and reasoning. What's really important in motivation is not actually the reward you receive but your expectation of getting that reward. If the reward is better than you expect, your dopamine increases. If it's less than expected your dopamine decreases.

However, dopamine, although it has a reputation as a feel-good chemical, works in more than one way. Gunfire isn't a reward, but it's a great motivator for action, such as ducking or running away. Dopamine is involved in both positive and negative motivation, depending on where it operates in the brain. It can move you either toward something or away from something. And that means that low-achievers can become high-achievers if they can teach their brain to release dopamine in response to positive and negative stimuli. It is possible because of a process called neuroplasticity, which I'll explain in more detail in Chapter 2. For now, just realize that you have it within yourself to increase your motivation.

While dopamine is important, there are also four basic drives that human beings have that can contribute to motivation and positive behavior. They are:

- learning
- bonding
- protecting
- gain

You can be motivated to learn new things and increase your knowledge base. You get a dopamine hit when you develop a bond with another person. You have a positive feeling when you protect the things in your life that give you positive feelings, such as your home, family, and even your values. And you're motivated to pursue rewards, whether they're short-term ones or longer-term ones.

Build Your Motivation

How do you do that? Here are some techniques that work:

Make your goals achievable. Big goals are all well and good, but it takes a long time for them to pay off. If you have more attainable goals or break your goals down into more easily doable steps, you'll get that dopamine reward sooner and more regularly. That'll keep you going until you achieve your ultimate goal.

Reframe your goals. If you can find a way to convert an extrinsic goal into an intrinsic one, you'll be more motivated to keep working toward it. For example, don't think of cleaning the kitchen as a tiresome chore. Instead, motivate yourself by thinking of how you can have a friend over for coffee once you do it.

Recognize your achievements. Do you keep a to-do list? It may be more beneficial to create a "done list." When you accomplish each step toward your goals, write it down. If you start to feel defeated, look at how much you've already accomplished.

Work to music. Listening to music increases your dopamine level. If you can't listen to music while you're working, listen when you take a break. A good playlist can pick you up and get you back on track.

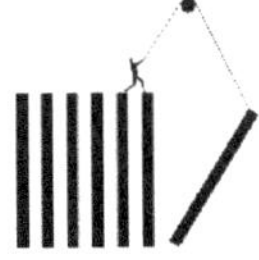

Key Takeaways

- Your brain's neurons and synapses create thoughts and memories.

- Learning depends on both nature and nurture.

- The brain sends electrochemical messages to the body.

- Fight, flight, freeze, and fawn are ways that you can react to threats.

- Thoughts are created in the brain and can influence your actions.

- Channel your emotions in a positive direction to drive confidence.

- Your brain is also responsible for motivation.

Chapter 2
THE POWER OF PATTERNS

We are what we repeatedly do. Excellence, then, is not an act, but a habit. –Stephen Covey

Human beings are creatures of habit. You do things without realizing what you're even doing or that your actions aren't under your control. But what if you could control them? The good news is that you can! It's possible to conquer bad habits and replace them with good ones. Once these harmful patterns are eliminated from your life, you can be healthier, more focused, and better able to get through your day smoothly. In this chapter, I'll take you through the process.

Habits and Behavior Patterns

Habits develop because of behavior patterns that you repeat. They don't have to be patterns that you think about; they can occur even without conscious thought. However, habits based on behavior patterns can be merely annoying or negatively affect your bodily processes. Here's a closer look at how it all works.

What Makes a Habit?

Psychologically and physiologically, habits are built based on the "habit loop," which consists of three parts. First comes the trigger or cue—the thing that kicks the habit into motion. In response to the trigger, you perform an action or behavior. Then, you get a reward for it—something that makes you feel better or satisfies a need.

Your brain is what controls the habit loop. It recognizes the trigger and prompts the behavior. When the reward comes, your brain produces a hit of dopamine, the "feel-good" or reward chemical. That's what makes habits so powerful. They initiate a good feeling. There are special structures in your brain that control this process. You can't get away from it!

Even bad habits produce a reward that your body and brain crave. Maybe every time you get bored (the trigger), you pick up a snack like candy or chips (the behavior). They taste good, and your brain produces dopamine (the reward). The next time you're bored, you're more likely to go for the snacks again.

Triggers are particularly hard to pick up on. You may think it's hunger luring you to that bag of chips, but it's really the boredom of sitting on your couch and watching streaming movies for hours at a time. If you find yourself scrolling mindlessly on social media, it may be because you're trying to avoid an unpleasant task like responding to a text from your boss.

Habits form rapidly. It only takes a few repetitions of the habit loop until a metaphorical groove that perpetuates the behavior is worn in your brain. Breaking a bad habit is another matter. Although you may have heard that you can break any habit in 21 days, that's not true. Some particularly stubborn habits, like smoking or ignoring your health, can take months or even years to overcome.

Conscious and Subconscious Habits

Some of your habits are conscious ones. You buy muffins at the store because that's what you eat for breakfast. You water your flowers as soon as you get home from work. The triggers are your thoughts—*I need to buy something for breakfast,* or *I should check my plants. They might be dry.* Those conscious habits or routines make life easier, which is the reward.

But a lot of your life is spent performing behaviors that you don't consciously choose. They're ingrained in your behavior through the habit loop. Terri Koslowski (2021) cites studies that say "habits, not consciously thinking, determine over 40% of our behaviors." That's a lot of your life you spend on automatic pilot.

Subconscious habits don't have to be bad ones, however. You can have good habits that you don't think about, too. For example, you might floss your teeth automatically after you brush them because it's part of your routine, and you don't have to consciously remember to do it. Or perhaps you always ask for a receipt, so you'll have them at tax time. You do this without thinking about it. You've done it so many times that it's become a habit. Again, these are habit loops: Your triggers are brushing your teeth and getting receipts. Your rewards are maintaining healthy gums and not having to scramble at the last minute to do your taxes.

The Power of Patterns

In Chapter 1, I introduced the idea that thought patterns are powerful influencers of behavior. They influence not only your emotions but also what you do. But it works the other way as well. Your behavior patterns have a significant effect on your thoughts and emotions, too. They can make you feel motivated, for example. The pattern of creating a schedule the first thing after you get to work sets you up for productivity and motivates you to jump into your day's work.

Your habits, both conscious and subconscious, and your daily behavior patterns have a profound effect on all areas of your life: your physical, emotional, psychological, and spiritual well-being; your beliefs about yourself, such as your confidence; and your success.

There are different kinds of patterns. For example, there are fixed patterns and growth patterns of behavior. If you have a fixed pattern, you perform behaviors the same way all the time. You might have a fixed behavior of always washing the pots and pans before you wash the dishes. It's not good or bad; it just *is*. It's hard to disrupt this kind of pattern. A growth pattern allows for change over time. Quitting smoking is an example of a growth pattern of behavior. You can change your pattern of having a cigarette several times a day by cutting down gradually. You can also think of behavior patterns as toxic or beneficial. For instance, binging and purging after eating is a toxic pattern, while maintaining a sensible diet is a beneficial one.

What causes behavior patterns? Some of them may be passed down genetically. More often, they're learned in your early environment. For example, if your parents and siblings have a pattern of keeping the house spotless, you're more likely to do that too. Your past experiences can be a factor, too. That's why someone who's been bullied often learns to bully others.

Patterns provide structure and consistency for your day and in your life. You don't have to think about the route home from work, for example. You drive it every day. The pattern of turns and highways forms a shortcut in your brain. You drive the route so automatically that your brain can do other things like listening to music or planning dinner. If your pattern is disrupted by a road closed for repair, your pattern is disturbed, and you have to use your brain to figure out a different route.

Your daily patterns also affect your productivity. If you have a system set up that allows you to get through all your tasks with ease, you can get more done in less time. Having structure in your life improves your mood and is good for your physical and mental well-being as well. Having a routine for regular meals, exercise, and sleep keeps your body healthy and your mind sharp.

Your Daily Habits

You probably have bad habits that you would like to change. They may be interfering with your life, health, or relationships. They may be simply annoying to yourself and other people. And since, by their very nature, habits are behaviors you do mostly without thinking about them, identifying your habits and analyzing them are good first steps to take in encouraging the good ones and changing the bad ones.

Identify Your Habits

It may be difficult to identify your habits at first. You may find yourself at first asking yourself; *Is this really a habit or just something I do now and then?* Answering that question is key. If you can bring your habits to the surface, you'll have an easier time deciding which ones you need and which you want to extinguish. But how do you do this? One of the best methods is journaling.

Journaling

You can perform this process by writing down your observations. You don't need to have a bound book with blank pages to write in. In fact, a formal journal may be too intimidating for you to use. A legal pad or a computer document will do fine. You can even use a pocket recorder or function on your smartphone to record your observations at the moment they occur to you.

If you find it difficult to write in a stream-of-consciousness fashion, you could create a chart based on the habit loop. It should have three columns labeled Trigger, Behavior, and Reward. It will probably be easiest to fill in the second column, though you may not even notice some behaviors like drumming your fingers or biting your fingernails.

If you're able to determine what your triggers and rewards are, add them to the chart. Try filling out your chart every day for a week. Do you notice any patterns? Do you see any habits that you would like to change?

Journaling Prompts

Your journaling can also be less directly focused on your habits. Try writing in response to one of these topics. Put the topic at the top of a page. Write as much as you feel like. Don't rush. Take time to think and surface your memories or sensations. Here are some possible topics:

- What do I remember when I was a child and visited relatives?

- What was the first thing I ever spent my own money on?

- Who was my first crush? Did I do anything about it?

- What was my favorite subject in school? My least favorite? Why? What feelings did I have during those classes?

- What games or sports did I like to play as a child? Do I play any games or sports now?

- What am I grateful for in general? What am I grateful for today?

- Who is the most important person in my life? How did I meet them?

- What is my philosophy of life? Has it changed over the years?

These questions may be related to your habits. For example, if the first thing you ever spent money on was a music CD or download, listening to music while you work may be a habitual behavior.

Are Your Habits Healthy?

People spend so much time talking about bad habits, but have you ever thought that some of your habits might actually be good for you? Health-related habits are beneficial, for example. If you go to bed at the same time every night and get seven to ten hours of deep, restorative sleep, your habit is having positive effects on your well-being. If you're in the habit of going to the gym before you head for work three days a week, that's another good habit.

Good habits can relate to any number of areas of life. In addition to your health, you could have good habits at work, beneficial habits of mind, or social habits. These might include:

- showing up on time for meetings

- thanking team members who help you

- laughing at yourself when you make a mistake

- keeping a gratitude journal

- practicing active listening

- validating another person's feelings.

On the other hand, most people have one or more bad habits. Here's a list of some of the most common:

- nervous habits like clicking a pen

- interrupting someone during a conversation

- being sarcastic

- eating foods with too much salt or sugar

- skipping meals

- slouching when you sit at your desk

Toxic habits are even worse. They can seriously impair your health, your relationships, or your job.

- drinking too much alcohol

- smoking or vaping

- binge eating

- overspending

- procrastinating

- losing your temper

How can you tell whether a habit is unhealthy or not? The biggest giveaway is that the habit interferes with your life or other people's lives. For example, impulsive spending can be harmless if you just pick up items in the checkout line at the grocery store or order a book or two online. When it gets to the point where you are late with your bills, however, you've got a problem with an unhealthy habit. If your habits endanger your health, finances, relationships, or job, you need to get busy and make a change.

When you realize it's time to change your habits for the better, start with the toxic habits. They may not be as easy to eliminate as some of the others, but getting rid of them will have the most beneficial effects.

3 Ways to Stop Bad Habits

Know Your Triggers

Examine Your Thinking

Desire Change

!

The Habit Loop

1 **Trigger** Stimulus Cue

2 **Habit** Routine

3 **Reward** Good Feeling

How to Change Your Habits

Can you extinguish your bad habits? Certainly, you may not be able to eliminate all of them, but you can work on them gradually. You might start with those that are merely annoying to yourself and others. Or you could work on the ones that are more detrimental to your health and well-being, since changing these will have the most impact on your life.

Control Your Brain

Habits start in the brain. Earlier in the chapter, I explained the habit loop that develops in your brain. It gets reinforced every time you perform a repetitive action. Habitual actions create pathways in your brain that store the behavior in your memory, making it easier to access without conscious thought. Pretty soon, you've got a habit. It's called experience-based neuroplasticity. Neuro-plasticity is the ability of the brain to grow and change. It happens quickly and easily when you're a young child, but neuroplasticity can happen in the adult brain, too. It's a passive, unconscious way of influencing your thoughts and behavior.

The brain can change on purpose as well. It changes to form a habit, and you can change the brain to break a habit too. The way to do this is called self-directed neuroplasticity. It's an active process. You take control of your brain and create new pathways that promote better habits. You do this by actively reflecting on your habits and how they make you feel. Unhealthy habits will likely make you feel bad, and healthy ones will make you feel better.

For example, if you get overwhelmed at work and need to take a break, you might start scrolling on social media and never get back to what you were supposed to be doing. You feel guilty for not doing your work. But the next time you feel that way, get up and take a short walk around the building. You'll feel better because you'll get some fresh air and increase your number of daily steps. You'll feel proud of yourself. Get used to the feeling—it's a healthy one.

How your body and brain interact to produce your thoughts, emotions, and behavior is complicated. It may seem impossible to imagine changing them, but it is conceivable. And it's important to be able to do that.

Here are some of the techniques that are most likely to be successful:

Substitute Habits

The best way to get rid of bad habits is to replace them with something better. Substitute behaviors can become better habits. Say you want to cut down on the amount of caffeine you drink. The obvious solution is not to keep caffeinated beverages in the house. Stock up your refrigerator with juice, sparkling water, and caffeine-free sodas (zero sugar if you also want to cut down on calories).

But what happens when you get to work, and the coffee urn is easy to access in the break room? You can also substitute healthier beverages there. Pack a couple of protein drinks with your lunch to give you that lift for mid-morning or the afternoon. Keep packets of non-caffeinated drink mix on hand that you can add to plain water for a refreshing burst of flavor.

Make Good Habits Easier

If you have a habit of forgetting your keys, you could be late for work or repeatedly lock yourself out of the house. If they're keys you use at work, you leave yourself open to bad reviews. The problem may be that you have a habit of keeping your keys in your pocket and forgetting they're there when you change into your gym clothes after work. Then, when you need them, you have to hunt all over the house, wasting time. Did you leave them in your car? The front door? Your briefcase or backpack? None of the above?

Set up a system that allows you to keep track of your keys. Put up a hook by the front door where you can see it. Then leave your keys on it as soon as you come into the house. Remind yourself at first that it's there. If you lose your keys, put them on the hook as soon as you find them, even if you're about to leave the house. Repeat the motion of placing them on the hook, and you'll begin to develop "muscle memory" that will help you get into the habit of placing them by the door where you need them.

Along the same lines, make your bad habits more annoying and frustrating. Habits are easy because they're ingrained. If you make it more difficult to do the behavior, you're going to eliminate it quicker. Don't keep fatty foods in the house. Sure, you could go to the store and buy some more when you get a craving, but that takes effort. That effort makes your habit less automatic. You have to work harder to get the reward and you may decide it's just not worth it to give in to the habit.

Break the Habit Loop

The trigger is what starts the habit loop. If you don't have the trigger, you don't fall into the loop. If boredom is what triggers your bad habit of "doomscrolling," stream some music you enjoy or engage your brain with a crossword puzzle instead. If you feel frustrated at work and respond by procrastinating, eliminate the trigger by doing something other than the task that has you tearing your hair out. Switch to another project or answer important texts and emails.

Make yourself accountable for replacing a bad habit with a good one. You could weigh yourself daily and record your weight to see how much you're losing. But that's frustrating. You don't see the effects right away, which doesn't reinforce good habits. However, if you have a buddy who'll encourage you and say, "Good job!" when you jog together or choose a salad for lunch, they'll help keep you on track. Write in your journal when you make it to the gym. Reread it the next day to remind yourself of how good it made you feel.

The point of accountability isn't to make you feel guilty when you backslide. It's to make you feel better when you succeed. It provides a better reward for doing a healthy action than the one you got from doing an unhealthy one. You'll get the dopamine hit from doing something beneficial.

Start Small

You may have a big goal in mind, but you don't have to tackle it all at once. Suppose you want to write a novel but feel stuck every time you see a blank piece of paper or computer screen. It's easy enough to develop the habit of calling a friend or sitting in a comfy chair, waiting for inspiration to strike. Instead, replace the frustration with a smaller, doable goal, like writing for 15 minutes or outlining one page. Sneak up on your goal by developing a good habit, one small step at a time.

Habit Stacking

You can also encourage a good habit by tying it to a habit you already have. Maybe you have a habit of making yourself a cup of tea when you're winding down for the evening. Attach another habit to it. While you're waiting for the tea to brew, wipe down the kitchen counter or start the dishwasher. If the first thing you do at work is consult your to-do list, find something on it that you can do easily or that's the most urgent, and cross it off. Nothing says that you have to tackle that list in order. Get in the habit of getting one thing done as soon as you get into the office instead of grabbing a doughnut or chatting with coworkers.

Visualization

Pro athletes and famous singers use visualization to improve their performance on the field or stage. You can use the power of visualization to start or improve good habits. As you're preparing your dinner, picture yourself rolling out your yoga mat and preparing to meditate. While you're driving to work, see yourself speaking up in the weekly meeting. You're likely to get a better result if you make your visualization as vivid as possible. Whether you're actually pumping iron or visualizing it, the same neurons fire in your brain and reinforce that pathway.

Cut Yourself Some Slack

Being too hard on yourself can turn setbacks into defeats. If you want to develop the habit of budgeting your time, but you get overwhelmed one day and don't keep to your plan, don't give up! Try again the next day. If you want to establish a pattern of going to bed at 10:00 p.m., don't be upset if you get involved in watching a movie and stay up later. One or two fewer hours of sleep for one night won't seriously derail your new pattern. Get back on your schedule the next day.

Going cold turkey on breaking a habit isn't easy, either. Sure, there are some people who manage to quit smoking that way, but most people don't. In fact, the Centers for Disease Control states that giving up smoking can take around ten tries (McLachlan, 2021). Perseverance is a good habit to develop, but don't take it too hard if you don't succeed the first time. If you expect perfection from yourself, you're setting yourself up for disappointment.

Healthy Habits of Successful People

A healthy body and a healthy mind are the best recipe for success and happiness. You get those by paying attention to the basics—sleep, diet, and exercise. All of them are benefits you can get from promoting good habits.

You may have heard about geniuses and millionaires who claim they sleep only three or four hours a night. That's the exception to the rule, however, and nothing that you should try to emulate. Sleep refreshes both your body and your brain. Getting 7–9 hours of sleep per night is the amount that keeps you sharp and healthy.

When you sleep, your body renews itself, and your brain goes through the process of REM sleep, or dreaming. Dreaming helps you process your memories and integrate them. That's why you sometimes wake up with the solution to a problem that's been bothering you.

What you eat builds up your body, but it also affects your mind. If you eat too much or the wrong things, you can put on weight and increase your risk of high blood pressure, diabetes, heart trouble, and even death. You can also feel tired and unfocused after a large, heavy meal. If you stay away from vegetables because you hated them as a child, you'll miss out on the vitamins and fiber your body needs to function well.

The best diet for good health is one that contains a variety of nutrients such as protein, fiber, vitamins, minerals, and, perhaps surprisingly, even some fats and carbohydrates. The nutrients you get from food supply your body with energy and the building blocks that it needs to renew your blood, muscles, and cells.

There are lots of diets that claim to be the healthiest, but it's best to avoid ones that concentrate on one food group to the exclusion of others. A combination of lean meats, low-fat dairy, whole grains, leafy greens, other vegetables, fruits and nuts, and starches in moderation is a good rule of thumb for better health. One trick that helps keep your diet healthy is to pay attention to the colors of the food you eat. A combination of brown, white, green, and yellow or orange foods like squash and carrots will give you most of the nutrients you need.

Exercise is also essential for both the body and the brain. You probably already know that exercise builds strong bones and muscles and improves heart health. But it also helps you sleep well and boosts your mood and brain power. Exercise gets your blood coursing through your body and brain. In the brain, it promotes mood-boosting chemicals and delivers substances like glucose that improve how functions such as memory work.

What kind of exercise you do matters less than the fact that you do something. You can do aerobic exercise that strengthens your heart. You can do movement exercises that improve flexibility and balance. Or you can do strength exercises that build muscle. There are many options to choose from, including simple practices like walking, dancing, yoga, or jogging; sports like softball or even pickleball; or strengthening exercises like weightlifting or using exercise machines at the gym. Try to exercise for half an hour several days a week for a start.

Key Takeaways

- Habits are created through a "habit loop" that involves a trigger, a behavior, and a reward.

- Habits can be conscious or subconscious.

- Habits start in the brain, so start there to eliminate them.

- Patterns of behavior can be beneficial or unhealthy.

- You have the power to break the habit loop.

- The first step in changing your habits is identifying them.

- Sleep, diet, and exercise are the most important good habits you can foster.

Chapter 3
TRANSFORM YOUR BELIEFS

If you believe you can, you probably can. If you believe you won't, you most assuredly won't. Belief is the ignition switch that gets you off the launching pad. –Denis Waitley

Your beliefs have great power. You probably realize that they have great power over you. But did you know that they have equal power over the world, both the one inside you and the larger one outside you? It's true.

Where do your beliefs come from? That's the first question to ask. They're a combination of what has come down to you through your parents, genetically. They also come from your interaction with the world. How you grow up, whom you associate with, and what happens to you all influence your beliefs. In turn, those beliefs influence your thoughts, your actions, and your opinion of yourself.

Some of those beliefs help you in life, while others hinder your development and your level of success. If your beliefs keep you stuck, though, there are ways to change them into something more beneficial.

Here's an in-depth guide to the power of beliefs and how they work in the world.

Why Belief Systems Matter

Everyone has a belief system, whether they realize it or not. You have beliefs about yourself. For example, you can believe that you're a good person or that you're deeply flawed. You also have beliefs about the world you live in. You could believe that the world is a fair place where talent and hard work lead to success. Or you might believe that luck has a bigger influence on whether you succeed. Those beliefs will affect your emotions, your behavior, and your outlook. Your beliefs can be either helpful or harmful. They affect your priorities and your choices.

Looking at Your Beliefs

If you want to determine what your beliefs are, you need to look at your thoughts, emotions, and behavior. First, ask yourself where your beliefs came from. Did you get your beliefs from your parents? Do you still believe the same things they do, or have your education and your life experience changed your beliefs?

For example, you may have grown up in a household with conservative political, religious, or financial views. And you may have accepted those beliefs. However, as you grew and gained experience, you may have found yourself questioning some of those beliefs. That's not to say that your family's beliefs were bad, just that your beliefs changed.

Examining your beliefs helps you understand yourself better. If you go through life without thinking through what you believe and why, it's kind of like you're on autopilot. Your beliefs control you. As you learn more about your beliefs, you're more able to choose your own path. You may have come from a household that was filled with anger and harsh punishment. But as you grow, you come to believe that you want to raise a family in an atmosphere of love and support. You've changed both your beliefs and your behavior.

Your emotions and behavior are activated by your core beliefs. When you encounter something that challenges or triggers a core belief, you usually react to it in accordance with that belief. It's more or less automatic unless you have examined your beliefs and tested them against what you find in the world.

Your Beliefs Affect Your World

That's how your beliefs affect your inner reality. But did you realize that they affect your external reality as well? That's right! Your beliefs can also change the world around you. You probably already know that your beliefs affect how you interact with the world, but they also affect how the world interacts with you.

Your Mirror on the World

Your beliefs about aging can improve your health, for example. Breines (2015) reported on a study in which middle-aged people with positive beliefs about aging lived longer and developed less heart disease than ones with negative beliefs, even when they had the same general health and risk factors.

Another good example is the "placebo effect." It's well known that a person who believes that a treatment, such as medication, will have a better outcome and experience more relief of symptoms than someone who doesn't believe the treatment will do any good. Also, if you are seriously ill and believe that you will get better, you're more likely to than if you have a gloomy outlook.

In effect, your mind is a mirror that reflects your interior beliefs. If you believe that the world is a dangerous, threatening place, you'll see the news and believe the stories of war and terrorism while discounting the ones about beneficial trends. If you believe the world is a good place and basically fair, you will choose happiness and create that reality. Your habitual thoughts will influence reality in line with your beliefs.

Examining your thoughts and beliefs will help you when it comes to recognizing how they form your reality. If your beliefs create a negative reality, it will continue that way unless you learn how you can change those beliefs to create a better world.

Your Energy and Your Goals

What is energy, and how does it affect you? One definition of personal energy is the qualities of mind, body, and emotions that keep you in motion. For example, at work, you might feel fatigued, overwhelmed, and inattentive. The remedies for these feelings typically involve not skipping breakfast, deep breathing, and avoiding multitasking. Those things are all good advice, but they address only a limited definition of energy.

Another way to look at energy is to consider the human body and what it's made up of. As you probably learned in high school biology, the human body is made up of cells. The cells, in turn, are power sources for the body and are made up of atoms. And physics tells us that atoms are made up of protons, electrons, and neutrons. When you look closely at protons, electrons, and neutrons, they're vibrating with energy. In essence, your body is made up of vibrations and energy. You emit that energy into the world around you.

Yet another example of vibration is music. The strings of a musical instrument, such as a guitar or a violin, vibrate at different frequencies, creating the sounds you hear. Even a drum creates sound waves through the air that you perceive as sound and music.

Maybe you've experienced the condition when someone stands too close to you, and you feel uncomfortable. That's because they're invading your personal comfort zone—the reach of your energetic vibration. People's comfort zones can be larger or smaller based on their vibrational energy.

Different levels of vibrations accompany different states of being. If you're vibrating at a low rate, you're likely to be experiencing emotions like guilt and shame. A higher vibration may produce anger and even courage. Lora deVries (2023) reports on expert opinions that say these lower vibrations correspond to a rate below 500. Love has a vibrational rate of 500, and enlightenment has a rate of 750. If you're able to change your vibrational rate—and you can—you're able to raise it from lower to higher. This will affect your mood, behavior, and ability to reach your goals.

A person with low vibrational energy exhibits qualities such as feeling guilt, complaining, having bad habits, lacking patience, having self-doubt, and being judgmental and defensive. There are also ways to tell when you have high vibrational energy. When the environment around you is filled with high-level vibrations, you'll find that animals and children feel safe around you, that people smile when they see you, and that strangers feel comfortable talking to you.

Low vibrational energies are associated with negative thoughts and beliefs, while higher vibrations go with positive ones. And, as I've noted, your beliefs affect the world around you. Achieving your goals is dependent on being able to envision your future self accomplishing them, which is caused by positive energy and the vibrations that go with it. If you exude negative energy, you're less likely to believe in yourself, which can interfere with your ability to meet your goals.

So, can you adjust your vibrations to a higher level? You definitely can! Practices such as meditation and gratitude are helpful. So are exhibiting empathy, finding your purpose, and accessing your higher self through shadow self-work. Shadow work means exploring your unconscious thoughts and emotions and integrating them to achieve harmony and wholeness. Your shadow side is made up of parts of you that you unconsciously reject, or the dark side of yourself. Shadow work involves developing both self-awareness and self-compassion, both of which exhibit higher vibrational levels.

Your Self-Worth

What is self-worth? It's your belief in yourself—the belief that you are deserving of love and respect. It's a measure of how you see yourself rather than how other people think of you. Your self-worth can affect many areas of your life, including your relationships, your job, and other accomplishments. In turn, your self-worth can be affected by factors including your health, your interactions with others, and your social status.

One way to get a handle on your self-worth is to ask yourself how you would describe yourself. Pretend that you're telling a stranger about yourself. Would you say that you're a good person? Honest? Friendly? Compassionate? Or would you put yourself down and say that you're not very successful or that you don't have many friends? How you describe yourself is a measure of your self-worth.

Self-worth is particularly important in regard to your relationships. If you have low self-worth, you aren't likely to stand up for yourself in the face of bullying or disrespect. You may blame yourself for circumstances that aren't really your fault.

Low self-worth is associated with depression and anxiety and all the things that go with them—poor appetite, problems sleeping, and difficulty concentrating. Your negative view of yourself means that you tend to focus on your weaknesses rather than your strengths. When someone compliments you, you brush it aside, saying, "It wasn't all that good," "I could have done better," or "Janet is the real expert." You always anticipate failure. You downplay your own needs and let people overstep your boundaries without objecting. Or you could find yourself always trying to please others.

If you have a healthy sense of self-worth, you believe in yourself and your ability to bounce back from any setbacks. You don't think that you're the best at everything; you see areas where you can do better. But you view your abilities realistically. New opportunities are welcome, and you have confidence in your ability to try them. You can ask for what you want and need, but don't give up if you don't get everything you ask for.

If your self-worth is on the low side, there are ways to improve it. One thing you can do is exercise the qualities you know you're good at or things you enjoy. If you have a good singing voice, you don't have to perform in public, but you can sing as you drive to appointments or wash the dishes. If you like building model train layouts, set aside a space in your basement to create them.

Another way to build your self-worth is to exercise and track your progress. Exercise is good for your body and your mood anyway. And seeing yourself being able to do more—do more situps, jog further, or make more baskets—will help convince you that you're capable of more than you thought.

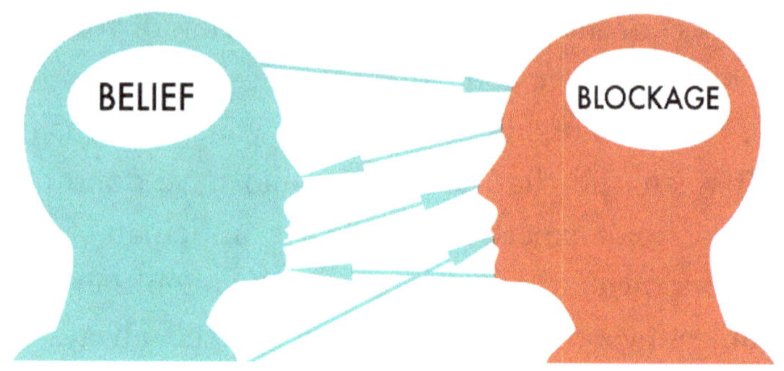

What's Stopping You?

So, if your beliefs can change your world for good or bad, what's keeping you from making sure that your beliefs make your life better? First, it's necessary to understand how your beliefs limit you. I've already discussed how your core beliefs are formed. Now it's time to look at the beliefs that harm you and how they do it.

What Are Blockages?

Blockages are what prevent you from accomplishing your goals and improving your life. They're also called self-limiting beliefs. Just like it sounds, self-limiting beliefs are those that interfere with your positive emotions and actions. They make it difficult for you to change your core beliefs and impossible to create the life you want and deserve.

Your blockages begin in your past. They grow from experiences you've had and messages you've heard throughout your life. Say you struck out three times in a row, and the other kids started calling you a loser. You may go through life believing that you're a loser or that you're just not good at sports. If your parents withheld affection from you, you may have grown up believing that you're not worthy of love. Those blockages are something your mind created as a way to understand what happened to you. Uncovering the roots of these blockages will not be easy, but it's important to do so. Learning how your blockages arose is the first step in getting rid of them.

Blockages get stronger when they're repeated. This may happen when the situation that prompted your negative reaction happens more than once or when it continues for a long time. Your brain gets stuck in a loop, telling you over and over that you're worthless, useless, or unlovable. When you hear that message often enough, you come to believe it. Those beliefs run your life and ruin it.

The important thing to remember about self-limiting beliefs is that they're false and not reflected in reality. For example, you might believe that you can never do anything right. That's not true. You may have suffered a reverse in business or gotten a bad evaluation, but that's not all there is to you. There are other areas of life in which you've done many things right. You may have been a good parent or a compassionate friend. You could be good at budgeting or working on team projects.

One belief that severely blocks your ability to succeed is "I can't do that." You're defeated even before you begin. Similarly, if you believe that you can't change, you won't be able to. Everyone can change, if only in small ways. You can abandon small bad habits like biting your fingernails. You can substitute an apple for a doughnut. Just because you don't make drastic changes easily or right away doesn't mean you can't change at all. You just need to start small and give yourself time to notice the changes. Gradually, you'll realize that change is possible for you.

Your Inner Critic

Everyone has an inner voice, also called an interior monologue. Some people think of this inner voice as the conscience, something that tells you right from wrong, moral from immoral. That's a religious concept, but it isn't the only thing that your inner critic does. Your inner critic tears you down by reinforcing your negative, self-limiting beliefs.

These can be large, comprehensive beliefs like "I'm not lovable," or they can be smaller beliefs like "I'm no good at math." You "hear" these statements in your mind whenever you experience a setback or are involved in a particular situation. The most basic things your inner critic tells you are that you're not worthy of happiness or that you're no good at anything. Those messages are extremely detrimental to your self-worth and keep you from accomplishing your goals.

Another common self-limiting belief is called "imposter syndrome." It's the belief that you are faking being good at something and that other people will realize it and expose you as a fraud. You believe you are never good enough at what you do, even if you have accomplished really good things. This overwhelming self-doubt is based on a false belief—that you don't deserve recognition for the things you do well. Many people who work in high-pressure environments have this belief.

Other self-limiting beliefs are:

- I don't have enough time (or money) to do this.

- This is too hard.

- I'm worthless.

- I'm not ready,

As I noted in Chapter 1, your brain repeats these lies whenever you face a new situation or experience, which creates a thought channel in your brain. This reinforces the belief. It promotes a pattern in your brain, making it even more likely that you'll hear your inner critic repeating it in the future.

Ways to Shift Your Beliefs

Transform Your Blockages

Two things to be aware of are the words "never" and "always." They're obvious signs of false beliefs. No one never does something or always does something else. In reality, you sometimes do or don't do them, or you haven't done them yet. Looking at your situation that way only leads you to negative messages and self-limiting beliefs.

If your self-limiting belief uses the words "always" or "never," challenge the wording. If your belief is "I never get my work done on time," say instead, "I didn't get my work done this time, but I got it in on time last week." If you think, "I always spend too much money online," challenge that belief by saying, "I spent less online this week than last week, and I can spend even less next week."

Also, remember the power of "yet." Instead of saying, "I didn't wash the windows," transform that into, "I haven't washed the windows yet." If your belief is "I can't do this math problem," instead think, "I can't do this math problem yet, but I'll get it if I keep trying." The word "yet" implies that you can improve and do better when you try again. The mistake doesn't define your entire future.

Confront Your Beliefs

Your beliefs may seem fixed and unchangeable—something that you just know because it's been true all your life. The truth is that they can be changed into something more helpful. This is not easy, and it won't happen quickly. But with some practice and determination, you can do it!

Changing your beliefs is easier if you question them like a lawyer cross-examining a witness on the stand. Lawyers ask for evidence to support their case or destroy the other side's. You can do something similar. Suppose you have the belief that you just aren't a funny person. Ask yourself what evidence you have to support that belief. Maybe you told a joke yesterday, and no one laughed. Ask yourself where the belief might have come from. Maybe your teachers punished students who joked around in class, so you weren't brave enough to try. Your parents might have watched all the news and cooking shows on TV, but never comedies.

Now think of other ways that you could be a funny person. Telling jokes isn't everything. You could find funny memes and pass them along on social media. Or print out copies of cartoons and pin them up on the walls of your cubicle. You'll get a reputation for having a good sense of humor. It may also be possible for you to get better at telling jokes. Get a book of jokes and go through it. Find jokes that you think are funny. Then share them.

Don't try telling a joke when you're giving a speech. Your nervousness will ruin your delivery. Try telling one in a low-stakes setting, such as a group of your friends, when you're out for drinks. Think about what kinds of jokes might go over well. Knock-knock jokes are for kids, but "dad jokes" are popular right now. A sophisticated audience might appreciate a good pun. It's best to steer away from off-color jokes and not to tell jokes that demean someone.

If you practice and don't get discouraged, if not every joke elicits hysterical laughter, you'll gain evidence that you can indeed be a funny person. What have you learned from the experience? You can be funny if you learn, practice, and persist. Those are good ways to attack any belief that holds you back.

On the other hand, you could also ask yourself how important it is for you to be funny. Maybe when you look at it, you'll realize that there are other aspects of your beliefs that are more important for you to work on. For example, if you believe you're not worthy of love or that you're a failure, that's more significant than whether you're a funny person. Work on confronting and changing those beliefs instead.

Visualize Success

In Chapter 2, I presented visualization as a technique to motivate yourself to accomplish your goals. It's also a good way to change your beliefs. It's hard to change your beliefs if you can't imagine yourself doing any better. If you can picture yourself accomplishing your goal, you're better able to do it.

Create a vivid picture in your mind of you doing whatever behavior you want to be able to do. For example, if you believe you can't keep to a budget, imagine yourself writing a sensible budget and planning for any unexpected contingencies. Imagine yourself sitting at your computer and using budgeting software. Then picture yourself seeing ads online and clicking right past them instead of clicking on them. Feel your credit card in your hand and the motion of putting it back in your wallet. Imagine the feeling of satisfaction when you still have money left at the end of the month.

One technique that will help is to develop a cue for the positive action that will challenge your belief. You might take a deep breath to remind yourself that you can do it. If you believe that you can't communicate well with your partner, practice visualizing talking to them calmly and assertively without getting angry or blaming them. Then, when it looks like an argument will develop, remember to use your cue of taking a deep breath. Use that as a trigger to begin using the skill you have visualized.

Exercises

Define Your Beliefs

How do you examine your beliefs and challenge them? Choose an area of your life, such as your relationships or your work. Then ask yourself questions like these:

- What do I believe about this aspect of my life?

- Who taught me this belief? Why did they do that?

- Were there experiences that caused or reinforced this belief?

- Is this belief helpful or harmful?

- How has it affected my life?

The answers to this kind of question will not come quickly or easily. You will likely have to revisit them more than once and think hard before you come up with answers.

Positive Affirmations

I'll have more to say about affirmations in Chapter 5, but for now, just know that they are positive statements that you repeat daily to make yourself believe in yourself and your abilities. Some examples of positive affirmations that challenge self-limiting beliefs are:

- I can do this if I try.

- I can change.

- I want to do better.

- I believe in myself.

- I am worthwhile.

Your affirmations can also be more specific:

- I can improve my eating habits.

- I am good at listening to my friends.

- My abilities get better with practice.

- I can do difficult things if I try.

- I don't have to put up with insults.

Now, create five affirmations of your own. Recite them daily.

Silence Your Inner Critic

A way to make your inner critic shut up and stop harming you is called "thought-stopping." When you hear the voice telling a lie about your personality or abilities, simply say to it, "Stop!" either silently or aloud. It sounds silly, but it works. It interrupts the pattern that your inner voice has created. Practice doing this until it becomes automatic. Then, replace the inner critic's message with a more positive one.

Another way to turn off that little doubting voice inside of you is to make fun of it. Give your inner critic a goofy nickname. You might call it your Inner Liar or Lying Louie, for example. Then, when you hear a critical, self-blaming message, you can just say, "That's Lying Louie trying to fool me. I don't have to listen to him."

Key Takeaways

- Your belief systems affect the world around you.

- Your vibrational energy has a great influence on your personality and your goals.

- Believing in yourself can change many aspects of your life, including relationships.

- You can improve your self-worth.

- Blockages, such as listening to your inner critic, prevent you from achieving your goals.

- There are ways that you can clear those blockages.

- Confronting and analyzing your beliefs is a powerful way to clear blockages.

Chapter 4
FIND YOUR PURPOSE IN LIFE

We are all capable of greatness when we know without any doubt that we are directly connected to a higher purpose.
– Andrew Cohen

It's possible to go through life without a goal or purpose, but that's quite an empty way to live. Having a purpose—or more than one purpose—in life gives you a reason to get out of bed in the morning, to improve yourself and the world, and to self-direct your future. A purpose in life inspires you, informs your work, and gives you a path to follow. It gives you something to aim for in life.

If you're unclear about your purpose in life, however, you're not alone. Too many of us simply drift through life at the mercy of the circumstances around us. But you can break free of that trap! Knowing your purpose is the first step in achieving it.

Finding Your Purpose

Why do you need to have a purpose in life? It benefits you in many ways. First, it gives you a focus for your energies. Purpose gives you a feeling of accomplishment and satisfaction. And it channels your best efforts into action that can improve your life. In fact, some scientists say that having a purpose in life improves your health, increases your longevity, and even positively affects your economic success (Suttie, 2020).

If you feel you don't have a purpose in life, you may be giving in to a fear of failure. In the next chapter, I'll go into more detail on how to face failure and triumph, but for now, you should know that it's possible to reframe your negative thoughts and realize that your strengths will carry you through.

Another reason you may not feel that your life has a purpose is that your own beliefs prevent you from discovering your purpose. Chapter 3 provides a detailed look at how your beliefs shape your reality. Now you'll discover how they can aid you in finding your purpose in life.

Your Personal Purpose

So, how do you discover your purpose in life? There are several techniques you can use that will steer you toward the path that will lead you to your purpose. Choose the ones that resonate with you the most and put them into practice. Soon, your purpose in life will become clearer.

Think About the Present

Before you can determine what your purpose for the future will be, it will help to think about where you are now. What is your situation? Are you satisfied with your path in life, or do you feel the need for a change? Can you see habits that limit you? Do you feel that you're stagnating, just going through the motions? Can you feel a desire for something more out of your life? Are you simply living up to others' expectations? When you feel alive inside, what are you doing? The answers to those questions will help you realize your need for a purpose in life.

Self-Reflection

As you might realize, finding your purpose requires you to examine your inner thoughts. Think about what you care about the most. It might be your family, your job, or your support for your community. It may not be easy to pinpoint one thing, as your interests and values may be far-ranging. Then, think about how the aspects you've identified are revealed in your daily life. Ask yourself if they affect what you want to do with the rest of your life. You can reflect on your purpose at any age; it doesn't have to happen when you're just starting out, though it often does. In fact, your purpose in life may change as you grow older. Your experiences can affect how you feel about your future and its meaning.

Use Your Imagination

Think about what you want your life to look like. What do you think your job will be like? Can you envision your future relationships or family? Imagine yourself 20, 30, or 40 years from now. What are you doing with your life? Can you see your vision of your best self acting in the world? Look deeper. Do you know why you expect the outcomes you see? And what do you need to do in order to realize your vision? All these questions can bring you closer to realizing what your purpose is and how you might reach it.

Consider Your Heroes

The people you admire have a lot to do with what you value and want to work for. A famous athlete may help you discover that your purpose is to pursue excellence in any field. Someone who spends their time and money on causes that benefit their community or even the world may inspire you to do likewise. An exceptional doctor may give you a desire to help people improve their health in some way. You don't have to exactly follow the pattern of your heroes. But you might realize that some aspect of their purpose in life reflects yours too.

Don't Rush It

Your purpose in life won't automatically appear in front of you. Implementing the above steps will take time. They require careful thought, and they may also need time to percolate. You should allow yourself time for the necessary reflection. And that means taking time for yourself. While you're wrapped up in your everyday concerns of projects and exams, your job, your family responsibilities, or your volunteer work, you may not have a moment to spare. But you need to find or make those spare moments. Take a day off. Take several. Keep a journal of your questions and thoughts and refer to it during quiet moments.

General Purpose and Higher Purpose

Your purpose in life is something that is within you and is expressed through your thoughts and actions from day to day. Your inner purpose may define your career or your lifestyle. If you've followed the advice above, you probably have a clearer idea of your purpose in life. But is that your only purpose? Could there be something more?

You may have heard people speak of having a higher purpose. By this, they often mean a purpose determined by their spirituality or religion, for example, a calling to a particular way of life. That indeed has a higher purpose, though it doesn't happen to everyone. But you don't have to experience a supernatural vision or revelation to have a higher purpose.

Businesses have mission statements that encapsulate both what they do and why they do it. Sometimes, these pronouncements are only attractive thoughts for public consumption. But a higher calling is a kind of mission statement that truly informs the way you think and live.

All human beings have a higher purpose, though they may not realize it. You may not be conscious of this higher purpose, but it's there all the same. If you are conscious of it, your higher purpose can not only make your own life better but also make the lives of those around you and even the world better.

Your higher purpose comes from deep within you—a profound conversation with yourself about who you are and what impact you have on the world. One attribute of a higher purpose is growth—your own growth and the way you contribute to the growth of others. Some examples of higher purposes are healing, delivering a message, and creating change.

Healing doesn't have to mean physical healing, though it can. Doctors, nurses, and other medical personnel often have a calling to healing instead of merely choosing it because it makes them money. Either they choose healing, or healing chooses them. Healing can mean emotional, mental, or spiritual healing as well. If you offer emotional support to friends in difficulty, you're a healer. Counselors and therapists can bring others to a degree of mental healing and growth. And religious figures, including spiritual teachers and inspirational leaders, can heal the voids that people feel in their lives, helping them realize their higher purpose as well.

Delivering a message can mean revealing a truth, but it can also mean something as simple as bringing information into the world, perhaps by writing or speaking on an interesting or important topic. It can also mean alerting your community to an injustice that needs correcting and helping to solve it. Teaching is a great way of delivering a message—not just facts but inspiration by example or by leading students to a deeper understanding of the world around them.

Creating change is another form of higher purpose. This can mean creating change within yourself, adjusting your attitude to be a more caring partner or parent. It can also mean spreading change throughout your community by taking advantage of volunteer opportunities or even contributing financial support to causes that also create change. If you have a new idea or see a way to improve things, you can fulfill the higher purpose of creating change.

Passion and Action

One way of determining your higher purpose is by looking at your passion, and one way of fulfilling it is by converting it into action. When most people hear the word "passion," they think of it in a sexual context. Of course, that's one definition, but in a larger sense, passion means anything that excites your mind and spirit, not just your body. Your passions are part of who you are and what you have done in life. And they have a connection to your higher purpose.

Find Your Passion

The first step in understanding how your passions contribute to your purpose is to understand what they are. What excites your mind and your spirit? What are the thoughts and actions that get you revved up? What occupies your thoughts when you're not concentrating on the daily routine of work and mundane concerns? That fuels your energies and your aspirations. There are ways to find out.

Ask questions. Even if you're just starting out in life, you have passions. You might lose yourself in a book or find yourself in the zone when you write computer programs. You could engage intensely with restoring an old car or lose track of time when you paint. It could even be part of a project at work that consumes your attention. Ask yourself what activities make that happen. Ask yourself what you're best at. What do you dream about doing when you're bored? What have you always wished you could make a living at? Those are all clues to your passion in life.

Look backward and forward. Think back on what you enjoyed most when you were a child. What kind of play kept you occupied the most? Something physical? Creative? Solitary or with friends? Children instinctively pursue their passions. Next, imagine you're 90 years old. What would your regrets be? What would you be most proud of? What advice would you give to someone younger? These questions can help you pinpoint what you care about most.

Make time. If these reflections give you a clue to what your passion might be, make time to do it. Experiment with your different ideas if you have more than one answer to the question about your passion. Try a few different things. Even if you find you're not absorbed by what you're doing, you have another clue as to what your passion might or might not be.

Forget about money. If money were no object, what do you see yourself doing? For now, ignore the fact that you have to make a living. Worry about how to work your passion into your life later. Let your imagination run free. If you could do anything you wanted, what would it be?

Convert passion into action. Passion and motivation are intimately linked. Your actions reveal whether you are following your passion or not. Try to pursue your passion, even a little, every day. Even if you don't actively engage in it, read an article about it or tell a friend about it. Don't let yourself be distracted by fear, resistance, or excuses.

Meet Your Higher Self

Earlier in this chapter, I discussed what a higher purpose is and how it differs from your daily purpose. Now, I'm ready to talk about your higher self. It's a concept that not everyone is familiar with, but learning about it has a lot to do with finding your purpose in life.

What Is Your Higher Self?

The higher self is called that because it is higher than the physical realm where we all exist. It's higher than your material body and the material world. It transcends what we call reality and the psychological part of yourself we call the ego. It's also called the true self, the authentic self, or the higher mind.

The higher self is a concept that refers to how you relate to the universe. Your higher self is within you and, at the same time, has a connection to the world outside you and even the invisible world that surrounds you. Although it's a factor in many religions, you don't have to believe in any particular one to get to know your higher self. It's a concept that anyone of any spiritual tradition—or none—can explore.

The higher self is often referred to as the soul or spirit of a person. The higher self can also be understood as your best self, the part of you that rises above the mundane and the everyday to experience something better and more inspiring. You can think of the higher self as the mechanism that allows you to understand yourself at a higher level. Whatever it's called, it's important to your functioning. Without a higher self, you would be confined to the physical level of being and miss out on the other levels beyond that.

Your higher self can actually communicate with you. It does this when you imagine, meditate, or dream. It uses personal symbols to embody higher concepts rather than presenting them to you in a literal form. Interpreting your dreams can reveal that your higher self is trying to communicate with you and what it's trying to say.

Get in Touch With Your Higher Self

So, if your higher self is trying to communicate with you, how can you communicate with it? First of all, it requires patience. Your higher self doesn't reveal itself in a blinding flash of light. It's more subtle than that. It also requires trust. When your inner self tries to contact you, you need to trust that it's something beneficial, not a demonic voice or spirit. Your higher self encompasses the best of you. The more you learn to trust your inner self, the stronger it will grow and the easier it will be to communicate with it.

You can find a connection to your higher self when your intuition nudges you. It can be a message that there is something you need to either explore or avoid. For example, if you meet a new person and instantly feel that they're an important person to get to know, follow up on that feeling. Maybe they'll become a good friend, or maybe you're going to learn something important from them. Similarly, if you feel uncomfortable when you meet someone new, it may be best to keep them at arm's length.

Mindfulness

Mindfulness is quite the buzzword these days. It's used in pop psychology, spiritual practices, and even improving sports performance. So, what is mindfulness? It means paying attention to what your mind is doing. First, you look at the stimuli your senses provide. Be in the present moment, paying close attention to what is happening around you—and inside you.

When you perform an action, search your mind. Ask whether you're doing it because you actively choose to do it or whether it's an automatic behavior. Think about the habit loop. Can you identify a trigger for the action? Hunger? Boredom? Frustration? Fatigue? Too many demands on your time? Running late for an appointment? A fight with your partner?

Finally, see if you can determine what reward you're experiencing (along with the effect of dopamine). You may feel satisfaction or a lessening of hunger. You may feel calmer or less agitated. You might avoid something unpleasant. Determining what the reward is will take some practice; it's not always obvious. That's where mindfulness comes in. Think about how your situation has changed since you performed the action. Pay attention to your body and the input from your senses. Are your muscles less tense and bunched up? Did you feel less nervous? How's your attention span?

Mindfulness Exercises

You can sharpen your awareness of the connection between your senses, your body, and your brain by performing these simple mindfulness practices.

Breathing exercises. Sit comfortably and pay attention to your breathing. Breathe deeply by taking in breaths that fill your lungs all the way down to your diaphragm. If you place your hand on your abdomen, you should feel it expand as you breathe in. Breathe out through your nose and feel your abdomen deflate.

Next, try "box breathing." Picture a square in the air in front of you. Focus on the top side of the square as you breathe in for five seconds. Picture one side of the square as you hold the breath for five seconds. Focus on the third side of the square as you let out the breath for five seconds. Hold for five seconds as you picture the fourth side of the square. Repeat the exercise five times or as long as you feel comfortable doing it.

Body scan exercise. Sit comfortably in a straight chair with your feet on the floor. Close your eyes or unfocus your gaze. Breathe naturally. Focus your attention on your feet. Feel the floor underneath them. How do your feet feel? Do you sense any pain or tingling? Next, move your attention to your lower legs and concentrate on them. What sensations do you feel? Do they feel warm or cool? Is there an air current moving past them? Then, move your attention to your thighs. Feel them pressing into the chair. Feel the solidity of the chair and the texture of your clothing against your legs. Concentrate on these sensations.

Keep moving your attention up your body, being aware of the bodily sensations you feel. Do you notice any thoughts popping up as you do this exercise? Don't fight them but let them drift slowly away from you. When your attention has reached the top of your head, sit for a few moments, savoring the sensations you have felt throughout your body. When you're ready, open your eyes.

Everyday mindfulness. You can practice mindfulness at any time, no matter what you're doing. If you're preparing dinner, put an item of food, such as a piece of fruit or cheese, in your mouth. Notice whether the food has any scent. Does it smell fresh or earthy? Feel the texture of it against your lips and on your tongue. Is it smooth or rough? Does the texture change as you hold it in your mouth? Now, bite into the food. Does anything change? How does the fruit's juice taste? Does the cheese release a pungent flavor or a creamy one? When you've finished experiencing the piece of food, continue with your dinner preparations.

You can practice mindfulness anywhere at any time. If you're walking in the city or in the woods, experience the sensations around you. What do you see? Hear? Smell? Touch? Taste? If you're driving your car, notice the world outside your windshield. What can you see? Do you hear music, a book on tape, or a knocking engine? Do you taste a breath mint? Is the upholstery a rough fabric or smooth leather? Experience these sensations, then let them go.

Meditation

Meditation is another way to get in touch with your inner self. When you clear your mind of noise and clutter, it's easier for messages to go both ways. But meditation isn't a requirement. Many people find the practice of prayer to be another way to contact their spirit or soul. If you decide to try meditation, there are a number of versions you can try. Here are some of the most popular.

Guided Meditation

Guided meditation is what it sounds like. Another person takes you through the process of meditation. They usually have you visualize a peaceful place, the sounds of nature, or another soothing sensation. Using a low, calm voice, they invite you to explore your imaginary environment and feel the peace around you. While you're in that peaceful state, your intuition may speak to you, perhaps telling you that you need to return to or find a place such as the one you've imagined.

You can find groups that practice guided meditation through a yoga class, or you can download or follow along with one you find on YouTube. You can also do guided meditation solo. Record your own voice-giving prompts, like the one below, or ask a friend to record them. Keep your voice calm and your pace slow. Allow at least 30 to 45 seconds between sentences to give you time to envision your setting.

Close your eyes and slow your breathing. Think of a place or time when you were happy. It could be someplace from your childhood, a vacation you took, or a place you would like to go. Stay with that image. Breathe slowly and deeply. Now, observe the scene around you. What do you see? Are you indoors or outdoors? What can you hear? Can you feel the air moving around you? Experience the sensations.

Notice the details. What age are you? What are you wearing? See the colors of your clothing. See the colors around you. Are you warm? Cool? Are you alone, or is there someone with you? Be in the moment and breathe deeply.

Slowly open your eyes. Continue breathing slowly and deeply. When you are ready, return to the present time and place. Notice how your body feels. Think about what message you may have received from your higher self while meditating. If you don't think of anything right away, that's okay. Carry the calmness with you as you go about your day. Revisit the memory of the sensations and emotions you felt.

Moving Meditation

If you find it difficult to remain physically still during seated meditation, you may want to try moving meditation. It combines the calm and focused mind of meditation with the physicality and energy of movement. You explore both your body and your mind. You focus on the positions of your body and the feelings you notice without judging them. Examples of moving meditation are yoga and tai chi, which combine attention on bodily position, balance and coordination, and breathing exercises. Other moving meditation types include mindful stretching, walking, or dancing. Again, if there isn't a group near you, you can find practitioners and instruction on the internet.

Another kind of moving meditation is forest bathing, also called eco-therapy. Forest bathing has its roots in Japan, where it's practiced in the many beautiful woodland and garden locations. In forest bathing, you slow down and immerse yourself in the natural environment around you. As you walk slowly through nature, you engage your senses. When you notice something like a tree, wildflower, or bird song, pause to take it in. Be aware of the sights, sounds, and scents of your surroundings. Move slowly through the environment and connect with nature. You can spend from 15 to 60 minutes practicing forest bathing, depending on your schedule.

Moving meditation has many beneficial effects. It reduces stress and anxiety. It energizes you and activates your immune system. Moving meditation leads to better, more restorative sleep. Keeping both your body and mind active can also combat the effects of aging. Forest bathing, in particular, increases less tangible aspects of life, such as a sense of awe.

Most of all, guided meditation and moving meditation can connect you with your higher self. As you focus on your body, attention, and breathing, you allow your higher self to take control and reveal truths that you can't get to through conscious thought.

Gratitude

You hear a lot about gratitude these days, and there's a reason for that. When you practice gratitude, you activate your brain, your compassion, your appreciation, and your sense of wholeness. When you focus on what you're grateful for, you gain a better understanding of your life. Your higher self guides you in realizing all you have to be grateful for.

Gratitude journals are the best-known technique for practicing gratitude. And they're a great way to surface feelings of thankfulness. But you don't have to just have a diary with a date on every page and write down that day's gratitude. You can do that, of course, and it's perfectly fine, but you may have an easier time if you have a prompt on every page to get you started thinking about the things and people you are grateful for. Here are some suggested prompts to get you started:

- Who has helped you achieve something important on a project or at work?

- Who has listened to you when you were feeling bad?

- Who took over for you when you were overwhelmed?

- Who has given you a second chance after you made a mistake?

- What art forms do you respond to? Which artists?

- What's the most beautiful place you've ever been to?

- What good memories do you have of someone who has passed away?

Here are some other exercises that will help you explore gratitude:

Countdown

If you're feeling particularly down, you may think it will be difficult to work up a sense of gratitude. That's the time to try a quick gratitude countdown. Starting at ten, rapidly name the things you're grateful for, all the way down to one. Think of it as a game show where you have to name the most instances of gratitude in the least amount of time. This really gets your gratitude muscles moving. If you want to, try the gratitude countdown with a partner, taking turns as you count down or timing yourselves as you count down individually.

Gratitude Letter

Think of someone important in your life—one who inspires gratitude in you. Why are you thankful for that person? Write a letter to them expressing that gratitude. It can be to anyone in your life, living or dead. Think of all the qualities they have that you appreciate and the things they've done for you. Write them in a letter. You don't have to send it to them or read it aloud to anyone. You don't have to mail or email it. Just read it over when you're having a bad day or when that person crosses your mind. It may be your higher self reminding you to show your appreciation in some way—cooking their favorite meal, for example, visiting them, or just calling them for no particular reason.

Gratitude Jar

Maybe you have a jar that you keep your spare change in or slips of paper with chores you need to do written on them. Instead, why not keep a gratitude jar? Whenever you think of a person, action, or object you're grateful for, write it on a piece of paper and put it in the jar. It doesn't matter if you write the same thing more than once. Be as specific as possible. For example, instead of just writing, "I'm thankful for my mother," write, "I'm grateful that my mother came to see the play I was in." You can take a slip of paper out of the jar from time to time and use it as a prompt for a gratitude journal or letter. Or count them up so you realize all the many things you have to be grateful for.

Key Takeaways

- You can think of your purpose as both a personal purpose and a higher purpose.

- Self-reflection will help you determine your purpose in life.

- Your higher purpose will lead you to growth for yourself and others.

- Discovering your passions and acting on them are ways to make your higher purpose benefit the world around you.

- Your higher self connects you to the universe around you.

- You can communicate with your higher self, and it can communicate with you.

- Meditation and gratitude will help you get in touch with your higher self.

Chapter 5
REALIZE YOUR GOALS

Your goals, minus your doubts, equal your reality.
–Ralph Marston

Identify Your Goals

Everyone has goals in life, or at least they should. Some people feel the journey is more important than the destination, but taking the path of least resistance can leave you wishing you had planned better. Goals are a roadmap that gets you where you want to go in life and defines the route to get there. Having goals is important because they determine whether you'll be satisfied and fulfilled. But how do you set goals? And how do you make them a reality?

Passion-Fueled Goals

In Chapter 4, I discussed finding your passions and your purpose. Those can be key when you're determining your goals. You have a better chance of achieving goals that align with your passions because you care deeply about them and are motivated to pursue them. Passion inspires you to do the work needed to make your life turn out as you imagined. It's a source of energy and enthusiasm.

Following your passions means leaving behind doubt and a fear of change. It's a key factor in having the resilience to persevere despite obstacles you may face. I'll talk more about resilience in a bit, but for now, just know that your passion can carry you through hard times. It can literally change the world and your life for the better. Think about Steve Jobs, the creator of the mega-successful Apple Computer. He followed his passion all the way from a humble garage to the heights of technological innovation.

Passion and goals create synergy. Your passions define your goals, and your goals fuel your passion. Together, they lead to success.

Realistic and Ambitious Goals

Of course, your goals should be achievable. Apple Computer has already taken over the world. That kind of success is something that only a few people, like Meta CEO Mark Zuckerberg or billionaire Warren Buffet, can achieve. What's achievable? Winning the New York Marathon probably isn't, but running in it is possible if you have a passion for fitness and sports. Becoming a CEO by the time you're 30 isn't likely unless you start your own business. But if working independently is your passion, starting that business can be an achievable goal.

One popular guide to goal-setting is having SMART goals—**S**pecific, **M**easurable, **A**chievable, **R**elevant, and **T**ime-bound. If you follow these guidelines, you're likely to create realistic goals. For example, if you're shy, a SMART goal might be to talk to five people by Friday. It's specific because you're going to talk to people, measurable because it involves talking to five people, achievable because it's not too large, relevant because it's a step in overcoming shyness, and time-bound because you have until Friday to accomplish it.

Another characteristic of realistic goals is that they're flexible. The future is not predictable, and you may have to adapt your goal to consider what happens in real life. For example, you may get the flu and not be able to go out and mingle with people you could talk to. You adapt by taking into account that you'll have to stay at home for about a week and shift to accomplishing your goal by next Friday.

But realistic goals aren't the only kind you need—you need to aim higher at times. Ambitious goals will take you where you really want to go; they're passion-fueled and less limited than SMART goals. They increase your focus and your motivation to achieve. Of course, it's important to define these goals in a way that makes them doable. Just saying, "I want to be successful" isn't a real goal unless you first define what being successful means to you. Lots of money? A certain job title? Good health? Stable relationships? You can't meet your goal if you don't know what it is.

One way to make your goals both realistic and ambitious is to have "stretch" goals in addition to your original goals. If your goal is to run two miles a day, achieving that is a measure of success. But a stretch goal might be to run two and a half miles. If you can't do it today, you've still met your original goal and can try again to achieve your stretch goal later in the week or next week.

The Goal-Setting Process

Once you've identified your passion and the general goals that are aligned with it, you need to go through a process of mapping out those goals. It's easier to do if you start with just one goal and work toward it.

Suppose your goal is to write your memoirs. The first thing to do is to write your goal down somewhere—in a journal, on a legal pad, or in a computer document. This has the effect of making the goal real to you and reminding you of it every time you see it. Pay attention to the language you use. "I will write my memoirs" is better than "I could write my memoirs" or "I want to write my memoirs." *Will* is stronger than *could* or *want*, and it states your goal as a positive intention.

Next, prepare a timeline. For example, resolve that you'll have a first draft by the end of the year or that you'll make notes for one chapter every month. This step promotes accountability and keeps you moving toward your goal. Another way to increase accountability is to have a way to check your progress. You don't want to let your progress toward your goal get swallowed up by the minutiae of everyday life. On the first of each month, look over what you did during the previous month. As you meet your accountability milestones, record them in the document you created when you determined your goal.

It also helps if you write down the obstacles you anticipate on the way to achieving your goal. For example, gathering documents about your early life from your relatives may slow you down. Or you may not get the first draft done by the end of the year if you lose your job and have to spend time looking for a new one, for example. Maybe you aren't comfortable with your writing abilities and want to attend a writing conference that will educate you. Some of these obstacles you can anticipate, while others will come up unpredictably.

Another way to look at your goal is in terms of the "W" questions:

- **Who** will be involved in meeting the goal? Is it something you have to do solo, or will other people be involved? You may need help from a coworker, a friend, a relative, a professor, or some other resource person.

- **When** do you see yourself meeting the goal? Is it something that has a hard-and-fast deadline, or is it more flexible?

- **Why** is the goal important to you? Which of your passions or values does it align with?

- **Where** will you find the resources, you need to meet your goal? Will you need to buy equipment or do research? Do you need to connect with experts?

Of course, it's good to have a grand, overarching goal, but when you think about it, it can be overwhelming. One of the best things you can do is break down your overall goal into smaller, bite-sized goals. These should be steps along the way that you identify as both necessary and doable. Make them specific, too, just like your SMART goals. Develop a system that works for you. For example, every day after dinner, I will meditate for 20 minutes in my study. Get into a routine. Make that routine a habit.

Think of the series of bite-sized goals as an action plan. If your goal is to increase the number of clients you have, plan on making five sales calls every day. Writing them down is important. Put "five sales calls" in your daily planner. Then check it off each day as you accomplish the action steps.

Stay Motivated

So, you have your action plan. But until you turn it from a plan into a reality, all you have is an intention. Intention means that you plan to do something. Action means that you actually do it.

It's good to have intentions. They mean that you have thought about what you want to do and have even planned for how to do it. But until you put that plan into action, all you have are your desires and the plan itself. You are no nearer reaching the goal you have set.

What's the missing element that goes between intention and action? It's motivation. The root of motivation is motion. When you put your plan into motion, you change it from a plan into an action.

Motivation is made up of several factors: how much you want to achieve your goal, the reward for meeting your goal, what happens if you don't reach your goal, and what your expectations are. Let's take those one by one:

- **How invested are you in meeting your goal?** It helps if your goal is not too vague. "Get healthy" is a good goal, but what does it mean? It's composed of many different factors—weight, diet, and sleep, for example. Pick one part of the goal that means a lot to you. "Lowering my blood pressure" is a specific part of getting healthy. And because blood pressure is a factor in cardiovascular illness, you'll be motivated to accomplish it.

- **What's the payoff if you meet your goal?** In the previous example, it's a lower likelihood of developing a life-threatening illness. If you meet a goal, you may gain satisfaction or some more tangible reward, like a better job or a published book. If it's something you really want, you'll be more motivated to stick with your action steps.

- **What will you lose if you don't meet your goal?** If it's a consequence you really want to avoid, like not being able to pay your bills, your motivation will increase. When you start getting late payment notices, it'll remind you of what's ahead of you if you don't take action.

- **What are your expectations?** Do you really believe that you can meet your goal? If you're iffy about it, your motivation will be low. If, on the other hand, you have positive expectations of meeting that goal, you'll be motivated to keep going for it. If you expect that someday you'll really run that marathon, it's a more powerful motivator than thinking that someday you might run a marathon.

Build Confidence and Resilience

Two of the most powerful qualities you can have that will help you accomplish your goals are confidence and resilience. Without these two attitudes, you're more likely to get stuck and not complete your plan. The good news is that these are qualities that aren't fixed. You can and should develop them both and make them part of your life and your goals.

Why You Need Confidence

Confidence is essential. Someone who doesn't have confidence has little chance of meeting their goal or even putting their plan into action. Confidence is the fuel for motivation. And it's a specific kind of confidence that's so vital. You don't need confidence that your plan will work as much as you need confidence in yourself. Belief in yourself will carry you through the sometimes-difficult stages of your plan.

Self-confidence is a belief in yourself and your abilities. You say, "I can do this" rather than "I want to do this." For example, you're more likely to quit smoking if you have confidence that you'll be able to than if you merely want to quit. This is especially true if you've tried to quit before but weren't able to. That can really sap your confidence. The trick is to encourage yourself to boost your confidence. You can say, "Even if I didn't manage to quit last time, I made it a week without a cigarette. I'll do better than that this time." You express confidence in your own abilities.

Confidence helps you break bad habits like smoking, but it also helps you meet larger goals. When you think you can't landscape your yard, you won't be able to. But if you have confidence that you can, you'll be able to. It may take a while. You'll have to work up to it gradually, using those bite-sized goals I mentioned. But if you believe you can do it, eventually you will.

You gain a lot from having confidence. It gives you the energy to pursue your goals since you aren't worrying all the time about whether you're good enough. It improves your relationships because it allows you to terminate a toxic relationship that's holding you back. If you recognize that you're worthy of happiness, you can do what it takes to find it. Confidence also improves your willingness to try new things. You aren't stuck in an "I can't" mentality.

Build Your Confidence

You don't have to stay timid and unsure of yourself. There are actions you can take to improve the way you feel about yourself and your abilities. It sounds paradoxical, but if you have confidence in your ability to increase your confidence, you're more likely to succeed. The following techniques also increase your self-confidence. Practice them regularly, and you'll start to notice a difference.

Focus on your goals. Instead of chasing a thousand different projects, give your attention to the ones that matter most to you. Wasting your time on someone else's priorities won't increase your confidence. Pursuing the goals that are guided by your passions will add to your sense of well-being and motivation.

Don't bother with comparisons. If you look at the successes that other people accomplish, you're not focusing on your own goals. It's particularly important not to compare your life with people you see on social media. You see only the good parts of their lives that they're willing to share, not the work and struggles that got them there.

Say no to situations that sap your confidence. If you know that an activity makes you feel bad about yourself, avoid it. Instead, focus on activities that you do well at. You don't have to avoid the ones that challenge you. Meeting a challenge is a good way to foster self-confidence. Just stay away from the ones that you repeatedly do poorly at.

Improve your skills. If your goals have to do with business, go to professional development seminars. If they're sports-oriented, find a coach or an encouraging buddy. Continuing your education, reading up on the subject you're pursuing, or seeking out experts can give you tools to make meeting your goals easier.

Act "as if." You may have heard that telemarketers are told to smile while talking to customers because it will make them more positive. Acting confidently can have a similar effect. Dressing for success really works. If you look successful, you'll have the confidence to be more successful. Choose a confident person you know and model your behavior after theirs.

Learn to accept the idea of "good enough." It's often said that perfection is the enemy of goodness. If you obsess over doing something perfectly, you never move on to the next step in your process. Letting go of perfection allows you to make progress, and that increases your confidence regarding your ability to meet your goals.

Know your strengths and weaknesses. Play to your strengths and minimize your weaknesses. When you accomplish what you're good at, you won't feel as bad about what you don't do as well. Of course, you want to improve in the areas where you're not as good, but if you obsess about them, you reduce your ability to make progress.

Celebrate your successes. When you accomplish an action step or do a good job, give yourself a pat on the back! You don't have to rely on outside validation to bolster your self-confidence. What you think of yourself is more important.

Affirmations of Confidence

Affirmations are short statements that you make to improve your confidence and self-esteem. They work because repeating them helps them become embedded in your brain and affect your thinking and behavior. It's thought that the repetition affects the parts of the brain that are responsible for positivity and rewards. Hearing messages about your own good qualities helps you believe that they're true. Then you can act on them in ways that prove them to be true. In essence, you're telling your brain that you are a worthy individual who can overcome difficulties and persevere.

You can write down affirmations, but most people prefer to say them out loud, which helps the message sink in. Often, people write their affirmations on sticky notes and attach them to their bathroom mirror, refrigerator, computer, or another place where they'll see them regularly. Whenever you see them, read them silently or aloud. Do this several times a day. For example, if you put your sticky notes on your bathroom mirror, say your affirmations as you're getting ready to go out for the day and when you're getting ready for bed at night. You can also put affirmations on your phone and schedule them to pop up throughout the day.

Lists and even books of affirmations are available, but the best ones are the ones you write yourself. They're more relevant to your personal situation and needs. For example, affirmations for confidence might include "I'm ready to meet my goals," "I can have confidence and success," or "I learn from experience and come back stronger." It may also help the messages be stored in your brain if you say your own name as you repeat the affirmation: "Dan, you're a strong and competent person." "Kelly, you accomplish what you set out to do." "Phil, you know how to make a good impression."

Here are some affirmations you can use to build your confidence:

- I have overcome difficulties in the past, and I can do it again.

- Overcoming challenges has made me more resilient.

- My goals are important, and I can accomplish them.

- What has happened in the past doesn't control my future.

- My hopes and dreams are within my reach.

- I refuse to be influenced by negative thoughts.

- I am proud of myself and always do my best.

- I can rise above fearful or angry thoughts.

- I will be productive today.

- Every day, I'm closer to reaching my goals.

- My past mistakes don't define me.

- I am going to make myself proud today.

- My actions are meaningful.

Write three to five of your own that are relevant to you and repeat them aloud three times a day. They really do work!

Why Resilience Matters

What is resilience? It's the ability to bounce back from setbacks and trauma. There are adverse circumstances in everyone's life, from everyday disappointments to serious events like divorce, job loss, a natural disaster, or some other dire circumstance. There's no changing that. How you respond to roadblocks demonstrates your resilience.

Resilience is a matter of adapting your thoughts and behavior to deal with adversity. It isn't just a characteristic you're born with. It can be cultivated and practiced, built up just like you build a muscle. You can grow into resilience as you experience life in all its complexities. You can practice your problem-solving skills and get out of your comfort zone. Here are some other things you can do to help in your quest for resilience.

Concentrate on aspects you can control. The primary one is your own reaction. You may be devastated, angry, or hopeless at first, but you can use the lessons in this book to change your attitude to one of resilience. Then there are circumstances that are within your ability to control. They may start with small steps—polishing up your resume, finding a new apartment, consulting a lawyer, or gathering resources, for example. These are the building blocks of resilience.

Prepare yourself. Since you know that adverse events are bound to happen, you can improve your ability to get through them by putting systems in place that will help you through. This could mean having important documents in order and stored safely, or putting money in a savings account in case of emergencies.

Make connections. Look for help from your support system and the people, support groups, and organizations around you. You don't have to go it alone. In addition, you can reach out to help others who are experiencing trouble. You can get your mind off your own situation for a while and get a boost of pride from being useful.

Maintain perspective. Don't imagine the worst. Remember that you have been through traumas in the past, and so far, you have survived them all. Accept where you are but hope for the future.

Prioritize wellness. Keeping your body and mind strong will help you withstand troubles. Letting yourself get rundown weakens your ability to cope. You'll be undergoing a lot of stress, so use stress management techniques to keep your mind clear and your spirit refreshed.

Remember your values. It's easy for troubles and tragedies to shake your foundations but maintaining them is important. Continue to act in accordance with your beliefs, and you won't disappoint yourself by abandoning your core values. If you value honesty, be honest with yourself about your situation. If you believe in the possibility of change for the better, hold tight to that.

Confront Failure

What if you experience not just traumatic events but some sort of failure? Resilience is even more important when that happens. Instead of feeling overwhelmed and simply giving up, you have the opportunity to rebuild and grow.

Learn From Failure

Failure is often an opportunity for a fresh start. It's a cliché to say that every cloud has a silver lining or that every failure is a learning opportunity, but there's really some truth there. In science, engineering, and industry, failure often leads to advances. If one idea or strategy fails, it can point the way to a newer, better one or a way to prevent making the same mistake again.

What are some of the ways you can turn failure into an opportunity? Here are some strategics.

Accept your feelings. At first, failure brings disappointment, frustration, or defeat. Denying those emotions isn't helpful. The trick is to acknowledge the way you feel and approach it with a little self-compassion. You don't have to wallow in your negative feelings but accepting them is the first step to moving beyond them.

Avoid unhealthy strategies. You may be tempted to isolate yourself because of the blame or shame you might be feeling. Instead, create an environment filled with positive people who can lift you up. You could be tempted to drown your sorrows in alcohol or drugs. These are just ways to avoid reality and are not just unhealthy but unhelpful.

Conquer irrational beliefs. Many people believe that just because they fail, they're a total failure. They say to themselves, "I'm not worthy of success" or "I suck at this." It's much more realistic to acknowledge that you failed *this time* and haven't succeeded *yet*. These beliefs leave open the possibility of growth and change.

Create a plan. Look at what you could do differently the next time you confront a problem that might lead to failure. Do you need to hire new team members? Improve accountability? Change procedures? Prepare yourself so that you can avoid the next failure that could happen.

Analyze and pivot. Figure out why you failed, and you're on the road to preventing future failure. Don't stay invested in what led to that failure. Try something new. It's like the old saying, "Don't throw good money after bad." Once you know why you failed, dedicate yourself to not doing that again. Watch yourself—you don't want to get caught in a nasty, unproductive habit loop.

Rejection as Redirection

Rejection is a very specific kind of failure, and it hurts a lot. The same parts of the brain that process physical pain also process the emotional pain of rejection. Besides, rejection taps into the very basic human need for belonging. When you've been rejected, you feel cut off from that feeling of belonging.

The physical, mental, and emotional effects of rejection are profound. You can feel hurt, embarrassed, envious, shame, guilt, fear, grief, anger, a longing for reconnection, or several of these emotions at once. If you've been "ghosted," you may indulge in overthinking or wondering what you did wrong. It helps if you can examine your feelings and name them instead of just saying, "I feel bad" or "I feel sad." It makes it easier to understand what you're feeling and move on if you can get specific.

Moving on is your ultimate goal. You need to heal from rejection to regain your self-esteem and lessen your depression. Here are some ways you can do that:

Think of rejection as redirection. Although many people grieve the end of a relationship, not being accepted by a college or at a job, or simply being turned down for a date, you can also view it as a message from the universe. It may be telling you that it's time to move on because better things are waiting for you.

Take your own advice. Imagine what you would say to a friend who had suffered a similar rejection. You can even write a letter expressing what you would advise. Then reread the letter and apply it to your own situation.

Try problem-focused coping. First, clarify your problem. Take a hard look at what happened. Then, list your options for dealing with it. For example, you might be able to repair a relationship that's been damaged. Maybe an apology is in order if you were partly responsible for the break. Next, list the pros and cons of your options and weigh them. Finally, choose the best option and take concrete steps toward implementing it.

Don't take it personally. Admittedly, this is difficult. Just remember, though, that rejection doesn't define you. Your sense of self may be damaged for a time, but with self-compassion and the practice of mindfulness, you can achieve a new understanding of the situation. You can also seek compassion, distraction, or understanding from your existing social circle. All of them have experienced rejection too. Everyone does! You may feel alone, but you're really not.

Key Takeaways

- Goals that align with your passions are ones that matter to you and that you're more likely to pursue.

- Make your goals both realistic and ambitious.

- Break your goals down into bite-sized action steps to make them achievable.

- Use motivation to keep moving forward.

- You can improve your confidence, which will also improve your ability to meet your goals.

- Resilience is the key to surviving when you experience difficulties.

- Failure and rejection are opportunities to learn, grow, and rededicate yourself to your goals.

Chapter 6
THE STRENGTH OF SELF

You yourself, as much as anybody in the entire universe, deserve your love and affection. –Sharon Salzberg

Two of the strongest forces in the universe are self-love and self-care. They have the power to change your life. They improve your mood and your motivation. They provide confidence and satisfaction. And they boost your mental and emotional health.

Unfortunately, not everyone feels self-love or practices self-care, despite their benefits. You can enrich your life, though, if you learn how to make them part of your life. In this chapter, I'll reveal the secrets of self-love and self-care—what they mean to you and what you can do to reap the benefits.

Let's start by examining self-love.

What Is Self-Love?

It ought to be easy to define self-love. Just the name suggests that it means loving yourself. But self-love is so much more. It's a state of mind and a way of living. Self-love means accepting yourself and celebrating your good qualities. It means believing in yourself and pursuing the best possible life that you envision. It's a spiritual quality but also a practical way of looking at yourself and your relationship with the world. When you understand self-love and harness its awesome power, you'll be better able to meet your goals and improve your life.

Self-Love in Your Life

You might be afraid that by practicing self-love, you'd be giving in to narcissism or self-indulgence. Nothing could be further from the truth. Narcissism involves thinking you're better than everyone else and that only your needs matter. It's a dangerous psychological condition that's hurtful to the people around you. Self-indulgence means giving into your every whim, whether or not it's good for you or those around you. It means being selfish and greedy, not considering the wants and needs of others.

Self-love, on the other hand, involves realizing your own true worth and appreciating your good qualities while acknowledging your personal weaknesses realistically. You don't need to compare yourself to others or tear them down in order to build yourself up. Self-love focuses on your emotional and psychological health and well-being. You take care of your needs and explore your potential. You treat yourself with compassion and kindness. In essence, you treat yourself the way you would treat someone you care deeply for.

Self-love is deeply personal. Every human being is unique, made up of qualities that belong to them alone. When you learn to love yourself, you are developing a closer relationship with that very special person—you! As you learn more and more about your individual worth, you grow to appreciate not only your own identity but the vast panorama of the differences that people demonstrate. You grow to view yourself as a vital part of life, precious and worthwhile.

What happens if you don't have self-love? Your mental health can suffer. A lack of self-love is associated with depression and overthinking about problems. It shows up in a number of other psychological problems, such as eating disorders, anxiety, and post-traumatic stress disorder. And those conditions are known to have negative effects on your physical health as well.

If you don't love yourself, you avoid challenges rather than facing them with confidence. You go on the defensive and risk being crushed by adversity. You find yourself in competition with other people instead of building stronger relationships, leaving you isolated. If you don't have self-love, you can easily lose yourself in self-criticism. You give in to internal messages that you're no good or unworthy. You beat yourself up over minor mistakes and blame yourself whenever something goes wrong. And that critical view of yourself leads to an increase in stress hormones, which affect your physical and mental health.

Other potential consequences of a lack of self-love include:

- fear of failure

- self-neglect

- toxic relationships

- a need for external validation

- self-sabotage

- feeling inadequate

The Benefits of Self-Love

So, if a lack of self-love can have such devastating consequences, what positive good can self-love bring?

Self-love can increase your empathy. As you learn more about your inner self, you come to have compassion for yourself and others. You identify with their struggles and triumphs because you see yourself in them.

Confidence is one of the most powerful effects of self-love. When you know and love yourself, you have faith in yourself, which allows you to act in ways that will get you closer to your life goals. Your willingness to take risks will increase. And those risks will be the ones that lead to a better life, rather than the potentially self-destructive kind. You'll have the confidence that you need to see how your life can improve if you stretch yourself. You'll believe in your own ability to succeed.

Self-love also means protecting yourself from unhealthy influences. If you really know and value yourself, you'll be able to say no to requests that might interfere with your health and happiness. For example, you can avoid getting into relationships you know aren't right for you.

Greater happiness and optimism will be yours if you develop healthy self-love. Your moods will improve, and your motivation will too. The difference in your relationships will be noticeable. Because you're able to see the good in you and love yourself, you'll be better able to see the good in others and love them too.

Self-love adds to a feeling of security. Knowing that you are worthy of love and respect will make you better able to deal with any insecurity you may have felt. You'll also be able to accept other people as they are, just as you have learned to accept yourself. And that will allow you to be less judgmental of yourself and others.

Profoundly understanding your characteristics lets you know what you're capable of. This, in turn, will help you set goals and do what's necessary to make them a reality. You'll have more energy, which will increase your motivation to accomplish your goals.

Finally, self-love can improve your physical health. How? It's been linked to better functioning of your immune responses and increased relaxation. Controlling your stress offers many health benefits, including a reduced risk of cardiovascular disease, migraines, and gastric difficulties.

Exercises for Self-Love

How can you explore and increase your self-love? Here are some practices that will improve your capacity for self-love.

Write yourself a letter. Pretend you are someone who has a close relationship with you, such as your best friend, your roommate, or a close family member. Write yourself a letter from their point of view. What would they say are your best qualities? When have they noticed you treating yourself with compassion? Would they say that you value yourself? How can they tell? Keep this letter and read it when you are feeling bad about yourself. Think about the contents. How did reading the letter make you feel about yourself? Do you feel better after reading it?

Practice meditation. If you meditate, consider what you love about yourself. Explore what it means to love yourself. Open yourself up to feelings of love for yourself. Follow along with a guided meditation on self-love. (There are many available on the internet.) Picture yourself as a child and give yourself the love you needed then.

Let go of comparisons. It's easy to feel bad about yourself if you constantly compare yourself to other people. Instead, pay attention to their good qualities and consider how you share them.

Don't spend your time thinking that they are better than you are. Appreciate them for who they are and how you like them.

Forgive yourself. Sure, you have made mistakes. Everyone does. Think about how you would forgive a person who did the same thing. Apply that same compassion to yourself. Notice when you are blaming and shaming yourself, and let go of those feelings. Replace them with understanding and envision yourself doing better. Congratulate yourself on your desire and ability to improve.

What Is Self-Care?

From everything you read in the media, you may think that self-care means bubble baths, shopping expeditions, and lavish desserts—in other words, self-indulgence. While treating yourself to small luxuries can be part of self-care, it's far from the only part. In fact, immersing yourself in decadence can be harmful to your well-being, which is at the heart of self-care.

The most basic elements of self-care involve physical, mental, and emotional well-being.

A Very Personal Practice

While there are some basics that make up self-care, how it looks will differ from person to person.

Caring for your body and your health is one of the primary practices of self-care. But how that looks will accommodate your current state of fitness and health. Sleep, exercise, and diet are the main components of health self-care, but an individual's needs will determine what they should concentrate on.

For example, in Chapter 2, I outlined what constitutes a good diet. That's still true for the average person. But an average person is difficult to find. One person might have diabetes, while another has high blood pressure. One person may be overweight, and someone else may be underweight. How they design their healthy diet will look different—more or less salt, sugar, protein, or dairy.

Similarly, a person's mental health will be personal to them. You could have difficulties being anxious or depressed. You might lack self-confidence or be too overbearing. You may have trouble maintaining healthy relationships. You might have a psychological condition like bipolar disorder or PTSD. The details of self-care will look different for each of these individuals.

In general, emphasizing positivity and allowing yourself to relax are good examples of self-care. That doesn't mean that you have to force yourself to be cheerful all the time. Feeling distressed or discouraged when you encounter setbacks is normal, and admitting your true emotions is better for good mental health than pretending you aren't affected by them.

What relaxation means is also different from person to person. You could find being on a soccer team relaxing, but it might cause your roommate to stress about winning. Maybe you relax when you spend time in nature, but your kids find it boring. You could relax by working on crossword puzzles, which could be intensely frustrating to your partner. You need to find what is relaxing for you. Relaxation is an important part of self-care.

Spiritual self-care doesn't mean that you have to belong to a specific religion or group, although the fellowship of practicing religion in a group can be part of self-care. But self-care encompasses many different spiritual practices. Discovering which one is right for you will put you on the path to personal self-care. Even if you don't practice any religion or belong to any faith tradition, your connection with the universe can be inspiring or comforting. I'll talk about spirituality more in Chapter 7, but for now, know that what you believe, and practice can form part of your self-care.

The Benefits of Self-Care

Since self-care focuses on physical, mental, and emotional well-being, it means you should improve your bodily health, focus on mental difficulties such as stress and anxiety, and learn to adapt your emotions to deal with a variety of situations. That may sound difficult, but the benefits are worth it. Here's a look at some of them:

Focus and productivity. When you have good physical, mental, and emotional health, you're better able to withstand the stresses that accompany work life. Your physical health affects your ability to do strenuous work and not give in to fatigue. Good mental health includes being able to focus intently without being distracted by intellectual fatigue. Emotional health allows you to deal with the negative feelings that distract you and make it difficult to work with others.

Connection. Self-care includes fostering supportive relationships with family and friends. Of course, those relationships go both ways. You have a need for support when you're having difficulties, but you also need to reach out to other people who are troubled. Emotional self-care allows you to do this.

Preventing burnout. Burnout is a pervasive problem in modern society. Carrying a heavy load of classes or having multiple work assignments or projects takes a toll on your body, mind, and emotions. Having good self-care makes you stronger and more adaptable.

Resilience. In Chapter 5, I discussed resilience and how you will need it throughout life. Self-care for your mental and emotional health helps you develop this quality.

Improved mood. When you're physically healthy, you feel better about yourself. Your energy is up, and your confidence is up. Mental health is intimately connected with your moods, and so is your emotional health. Making sure that all three are considered will result in greater positivity and more stability.

Managing stress. Stress is a killer. Anything you can do to lessen your stress will be beneficial, and all areas of self-care impact stress. Good physical, mental, and emotional health will all help you shake off stress and keep it from beating you in the future.

How to Practice Self-Care

With all the benefits that self-care offers, it pays you to focus on self-care. But aside from eating well, focusing on restorative sleep, and exercising regularly, what can you do to promote self-care? Here are some suggestions.

Schedule time for self-care. If you're making self-care a priority, it won't be last on your to-do list. Be sure to make time for rest and relaxation every week—every day, if possible. Put aside 15 minutes a day for meditation. Read a chapter in a book or a magazine article every week. Don't waste vacation time with a staycation that turns into nothing but chores. Do something that will refresh you.

Practice gratitude. Remind yourself of all you have to be thankful for, and you'll improve your mood. Keep a gratitude journal and write in it regularly. If you're feeling low, go back and read it to remind you of what's good in your life.

Indulge your passions. Make art. Make music. Go camping. Go birdwatching. Plant a garden. Join a book group. Do anything that relaxes you and makes you happy. This is especially important if you've let these pursuits slide. Not only will they allow you to relax and refresh, but they'll also lift your spirit and nurture your soul.

Be social. You don't have to be a social butterfly or be the life of every party. But do get out among people and interact with them. Have coffee and a conversation with a romantic prospect. Have drinks with your coworkers. Volunteer at the local animal shelter or food pantry. Get out among other people at a street fair or art show. Such interactions are stimulating and good for you.

Get a pet. Dogs are good for your physical health because they need to be walked every day. Cats are good for your emotional health because you can pet them, and they purr. Even taking care of birds or fish is good for you because you're involving yourself in the care of another living creature.

Take a digital detox. Electronics are everywhere these days, and they're a total time sink. You could be using the time you spend scrolling through news, memes, or videos for a more relaxing or energizing activity.

Pamper yourself. As long as you don't overdo it or use it as your only form of self-care, go ahead and indulge yourself in something that makes you feel better. Spend a little time on yourself instead of always taking care of other people and tasks. Set aside an afternoon to recharge yourself. You don't have to spend a lot of money to do this. You can bake yourself a chocolate cake or take a luxurious hot bath surrounded by candles. Be creative!

What Is Self-Love?

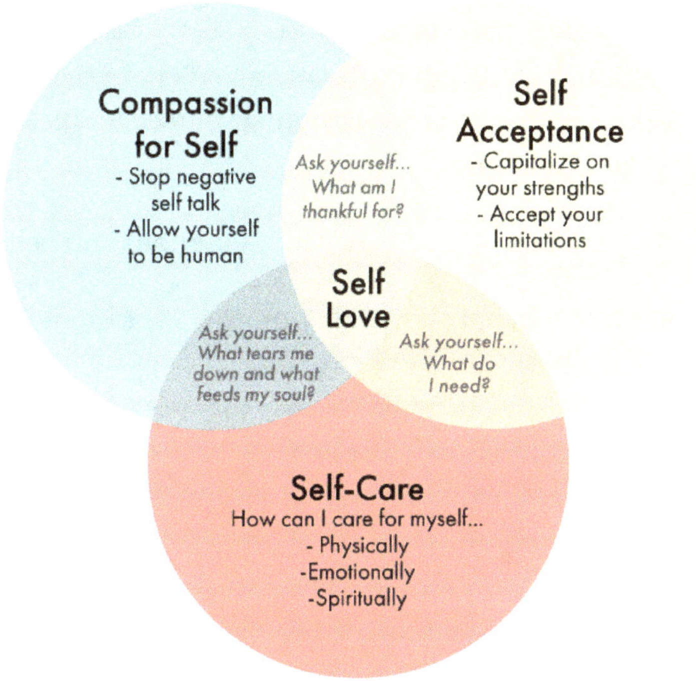

Key Takeaways

- Self-love is important for accepting yourself and celebrating your good qualities.

- Self-love helps you avoid negative emotions and behaviors.

- Confidence, happiness, and optimism are fostered by self-love.

- Self-love makes you more aware that you are worthy of love and respect from others.

- Self-care involves your physical, mental, and emotional health.

- Self-care can involve spiritual qualities as well.

- Social interactions will help improve your self-care practices.

Chapter 7
YOUR LIMITLESS POTENTIAL

To understand the precise point when the possible becomes the impossible, you have to appreciate and understand the laws of physics. –Michio Kaku

You may have bad memories of physics from high school if you have any memories of it at all. I've got news for you, though. There's an aspect of physics they didn't teach in school—how physics relates to your life, your spirituality, and your place in the universe. That's a lot more important than plasma and non-Newtonian fluids. When was the last time that impacted your life?

Follow along, and I'll give you a tour of new aspects of the universe that are actually relevant for you!

The Quantum Secret

Of all the aspects of physics, the newest and most studied is the quantum universe. Even those who study quantum mechanics admit that there's a lot they still have to learn. And for the average person, it's intimidating to think about topics like quantum superposition. But within all that remains unknown about quantum theory, there are principles that have meaning for you and your life.

Life at the Quantum Level

One of the principles of quantum theory is action at a distance, or quantum entanglement. This means that what happens in one part of the universe affects what happens somewhere else—even at a great distance. An elementary particle can be intimately linked with others at different places at the same time. Given the vast reaches of the universe, there are probably particles at vast distances that are linked to particles right here on Earth.

On a more personal level, consciousness is still not well understood. In the previous chapters, I've discussed how the brain produces thoughts and emotions. But consciousness is a different topic. Human beings, and perhaps other animals, are aware of themselves. They perceive phenomena and interpret the world around them. The mind can even contemplate itself, as we've done throughout this book. Awareness is the defining principle of mental functioning.

But how do you acquire awareness? Is it something that's within you when you're born? Does it emerge as your brain grows and develops? When are you aware of your own consciousness? And how does it even arise?

Fernandez (2022) reports "Some scientists suspect that quantum processes, including entanglement, might help us explain the brain's enormous power, and its ability to generate consciousness." Quantum mechanisms help explain how the brain interprets the inputs it gets from your senses. Observing how this happens is still a problem, though. According to the theory of quantum superposition, you can't know the true nature of a particle if you can see it. This is also called the observer effect. As soon as you see an electron, for example, it becomes either a wave or a particle, but not both. Its nature is determined at the moment you observe it. Until then, it exists as both a wave and a particle.

Another aspect of quantum physics that has great significance for the world around you is the subject of vibrational energy. This theory is based on two principles: That "the basic constituent of everything is the quantum vibrational field, which carries matter, energy, and information, and that "an object absorbs quantum vibrations through resonance. The reception and processing of vibrations—including information, energy, and matter—lead to subjective conscious experience" (Zhi and Xiu, 2023). In this understanding, the universe consists of matter, energy, and information that exist as waves in a quantum vibrational field. These quantum vibrations extend throughout space and time. When something absorbs those vibrational resonance waves, it results in consciousness.

The upshot of all this research and theorizing is that the brain may be a much more complex system than previously thought. Of course, the way the brain uses neurons, synapses, neuro-transmitters, hormones, and feedback loops is complicated and fascinating, but the quantum world hints at so much more than we've already learned. Maybe someday we'll gain an even better, more thorough understanding of how the brain operates and how thoughts and emotions affect the outside world. Until then, scientists studying quantum theory continue to discover strange new aspects of the universe within you.

Spirituality and Quantum Physics

If you're talking about tiny particles and the vastness of the universe, it can be hard to see how quantum physics is related to the deeply personal subject of spirituality. After all, spirituality is individual to every person and not part of any physical system that we know of. But that may not necessarily be true. Quantum physics may have an important role to play in personal spirituality as well.

Understandings based on material physics and psychology may be too limiting.

Classically, the world was thought to be made up of matter only. Everything that was physical and solid was real. Technology, medicine, and other physical sciences benefited greatly from this outlook. Tremendous progress has been made in these fields, and they have brought essential inventions to the world. Our lives have all improved because of this point of view.

But, from the material point of view, everything else was irrelevant. Subjects such as ethics, the arts, and spirituality were nonmaterial and therefore lesser disciplines, not worthy of study. Since that time, science and religion have been viewed as opposing forces. If you believed in one, you couldn't believe in the other. There's still a lot of this kind of thinking, and the two points of view are seldom encompassed in a single worldview.

Psychologist Carl Jung, however, said that there were forms and archetypes beyond the material. Imagination, perception, and thinking were just as real as matter. Another of Jung's theories was synchronicity, the idea that coincidences are connected in a unified system.

Jung's theories mesh with the theories of quantum physics because the quantum world is made up of things you can't see. Therefore, "the world now appears to us as an undivided wholeness, in which all things and people are interconnected, and consciousness is a cosmic property" (Ponte and Schäfer, 2013). Cosmic consciousness is an essential underpinning of spirituality. Denying this aspect of your nature can damage your spiritual well-being.

Because of quantum entanglement, you can remain connected to people, other beings, and places far from you. Quantum super-position suggests that there may be another point of view that combines both matter (particles) and energy (waves or vibrations). Not being identifiable in the brain, consciousness exists outside of matter. Quantum physics sees the universe as one system made of both material and immaterial.

Of course, spirituality feels like an inner phenomenon. It's not objective in the way science is and, therefore, cannot be disproved. As noted astronomer and science educator Carl Sagan said, "Science is not only compatible with spirituality; it is a profound source of spirituality" (Carl Sagan Quotes, 2019).

Many ancient practices of spirituality have recognized the profound connection between the personal and the universal. Buddhism, Hinduism, Native religions, Shamanism, paganism, and "New Age" forms of spirituality rely on the kinds of connections that quantum mechanics postulates. Even Christianity is profoundly spiritual, refuting the idea that God has a single nature but is rather three-in-one. Believers may not express this in terms of quantum mechanics, but the new breed of scientists might.

So, if you believe in astral projection, mysticism, reincarnation, destiny, oneness, channeling, and other spiritual practices and philosophies, you should feel validated that not all science and scientists deny your perception of reality. There's room for more than one view of the universe.

You and the Universe

Speaking of the universe, you have a unique relationship with it. Everyone does. The universe is vast, bigger than you or I can imagine. Scientists have a figure for how old it is, but how big it is, is still a subject of debate. They don't know how much matter is in it or what some of that matter consists of.

They're discovering more and more about it every day, though. They've located and seen black holes, which used to be theoretical. They've found other planets around other stars, including ones that have the right conditions for life to exist. Even with regard to the planets and the moons in our own solar system, there's a lot that scientists are still learning. There's no shortage of mysteries. So, are we alone in the universe? Almost certainly not!

Perspectives on the Universe

How do you relate to this universe? There's a lot we still don't know, but there's also a lot we do. And one of the things we know is that we're an awesome part of what may be an infinite series of universes.

The universe is so overwhelmingly large that we don't yet know everything that exists in it. But it's also possible that as vast as the universe is, there's much more to it than we realize. In fact, there may be an infinite number of universes. This is called the multiverse. There are different theories about what the multiverse might be like.

It could be that there are an infinite number of universes. The quantum theory I explored with you suggests that an electron, one of the basic building blocks of matter, can exist in any number of possible spaces. There are many different realities, and the electron occupies a different location in each of them. This isn't just a fairytale, either. The equations that predict the many worlds theory have been intensively studied and are accurate. They've been tested, and they apply to both the realms of the smallest and the largest scales of the universe.

Another way the multiverse can happen is called the bubble theory. It relates to the Big Bang, the infinitely large explosion that created the universe and all the matter in it. The universe expanded mind-bogglingly quickly and is, in fact, still expanding as well as cooling down. It's called inflation. But even as the universe inflates, it may still be only a smaller bubble in a series of bubble universes, all of which are expanding. What we know as our universe is only one of this infinite series of expanding bubbles.

The Nature of the Universe

Just being able to think about our universe and the potential multiverse means that you are part of something much larger than yourself. In fact, in many very real ways, you and the universe are one.

First, there's the composition of your body. It starts with the stars. Hydrogen and helium make up the fuel for the sun and the stars. As the stars get older, the elements in the stars undergo nuclear fusion that creates other elements, including those essential for life. As Carl Sagan put it, "the nitrogen in our DNA, the calcium in our teeth, the iron in our blood, the carbon in our apple pies were made in the interiors of collapsing stars. We are made of starstuff" (Carl Sagan Quotes, 2019). The substance that makes up your body regenerates approximately every ten years, using more starstuff. You rely on the element oxygen for life, and that's one of the elements that stars create, and plants circulate throughout the world. It's an awesome truth to contemplate.

Life began on earth from what's called the "primordial soup" of these elements; perhaps because of a lightning strike or another form of energy, a tiny, single-celled organism formed. We all share a biological heritage coming from those primordial single-celled organisms, which explains the similarities among all the creatures on earth. We are all carbon-based life forms, and we all take in oxygen. Even fish rely on oxygen that exists in the water, and they process it through their gills.

Beyond that, there's consciousness itself. You are aware of the universe as a living, thinking part of it. Your senses create qualities of the universe like color. The basic building blocks of the universe, like positrons, neutrons, and electrons, have no color. Scientists perceive the expansion of the universe in terms called red shift and blue shift, but really those are only measures of speed and direction. Even common objects on earth, like flowers and flamingos, don't have any color until light hits them, enters your eyes, gets transmitted to your brain, and is perceived as color.

The brain, which allows you to experience the universe, doesn't perceive it in physical terms, either. Your thoughts, perceptions, memories, and dreams don't exist as physical things. Your consciousness, your awareness of the universe itself, isn't physical. Your brain experiences electrical impulses that can't be seen either. But they enable you to think about the universe and your place in it.

Then there's the soul, or spirit. You can't see it or touch it, but few people deny that it exists. There are many different beliefs about the soul, but the most basic one is that the soul is part of you that exists beyond your body and your brain and beyond your existence on Earth. It's theorized that when your body dies, your soul continues to exist on some other level of the universe, whether that's called heaven, the infinite, or the mind of God. The soul may enter another realm entirely or be reborn into the world in another body, which can also contemplate the universe.

There's also the Gaia Hypothesis. It says that the Earth and everything within it are part of a giant, interconnected system. Living and nonliving parts of the Earth interact to create a biosphere that regulates everything on the planet. It's been compared to one large, living organism. Self-regulatory feedback loops keep everything on Earth in a condition favorable to life. In this view, the Earth is a single living entity. The Gaia Hypothesis describes a broad, interdisciplinary system and has many believers.

Some physicists are even beginning to speak of a conscious universe, one that participates in our awareness and consciousness. In this view, consciousness is a factor in every part of nature. When you understand that you and the universe are one, you have a more profound view of your place in existence and the universe's place in you.

Look Within Yourself

I've just been helping you to look outward at the stars and the universe and how they are connected to you and all life on Earth. I've encouraged you to look both outward and inward to see what you're made of, both physically and metaphysically. Now it's time to explore the reality of your life and your future further. How you view yourself has a vast effect on your ability to realize your unique potential and achieve all that you desire in life.

Recognizing Your Potential

The word "potential" refers to the possibilities that are part of your being. It means the qualities within you that can help you grow and develop into something better than you are. Your potential and how you use it define your future success and happiness. If you fulfill your potential, you can become the best version of yourself.

You often hear stories about people with physical or mental disabilities who are able to reach their full potential by overcoming their limitations. But all of us have limitations. Most of them are self-imposed. You think you can't do something, so you can't. To recognize your potential, you have to understand what you think of as limitations and find a way to neutralize them.

Mindset and motivation are the keys to unlocking your limitless potential. I've detailed some of the ways you can cultivate your real potential. Mindfulness, guided and moving meditation, affirmation, journaling, visualization, breathing exercises, goal-setting, and self-care have all been explained and explored.

Your potential isn't something that's fixed. You can affect how it develops—and how you reach it—through any number of practices. They include:

- **Gratitude.** Being grateful for what you already have is a good basis for becoming what you can be. Keeping a gratitude journal is a popular recommendation.

- **Energy healing.** Explore complementary and alternative methods of healing such as reiki, acupuncture, healing touch, yoga, massage, aromatherapy, movement therapy, and qigong.

- **Open your chakras.** The seven chakras are energy centers that run through the body. If they're blocked, you can experience physical and emotional symptoms. Yoga, breathing exercises, and meditation are all ways to unblock them.

- **Build intuition.** Your intuition can put you in touch with the world inside you and around you. Experiment with following your intuition and see where it leads you.

- **Keep an open mind.** Explore new ideas and fresh perspectives. Questioning and challenging the beliefs you hold can open you to new ways of being.

- **Get feedback.** Learn from someone who is further along the path to fulfilled potential than you are. Use their experience and wisdom to guide you.

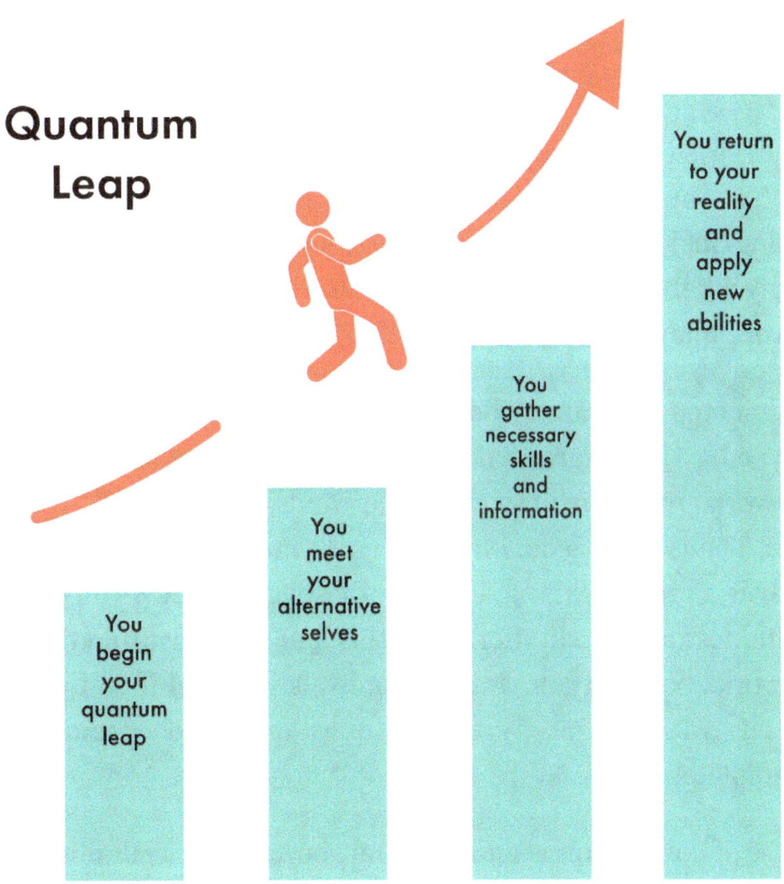

Make Your Quantum Leap!

The spiritual meaning of a quantum leap is a sudden internal or personal shift in consciousness that can occur after a life-changing event or decision, or even something as subtle as reading a book or finding inspiration in a dream. A quantum leap is when you jump from one energy state to another. It's like going from the ground floor to the penthouse in one giant bound.

In other words, a quantum leap is a sudden change from one state of being to another. You change from the state of being ego-driven and separate from your source to another level, spirit-led, connected to the vibrations of the universe.

Physics says that you are part of the Earth, the stars, and even the universe! Therefore, they are part of you, too. Everything you need is living inside you. It's your mission to look inside yourself, identify what you need, and bring it out. When you do, you'll find that your quantum leap is ready to happen.

The first step in finding what you need is knowing yourself. To do this, you have to ignore all the distractions that surround you every day: work, relationships, chores, errands, and especially social media. That's hard to do. Making time to meet yourself calmly and quietly is a precious thing. I've already suggested how you can use mindfulness and meditation to do this, but you must find the path that works best for you. Journaling is also helpful if you provide yourself with deep, revealing questions and prompts to contemplate.

A sense of connection is another vital source. Connection with the universe is possible, and so is connection with your immediate surroundings. Think about what you need most in your life. Is it peace? Love? Honesty? Are these qualities lacking or abundant? There is at least a seed or a possibility of them within you. Nurture those seeds and explore those possibilities to bring them into your reality.

If you're having difficulty identifying the qualities within you or bringing them to the surface, look for a mentor who can help you find your inner needs. This can be a guide or a life coach. Choose someone who has experience assisting people in answering their central questions and providing helpful feedback.

Finding yourself and manifesting what you need isn't necessarily a head-in-the-clouds procedure. It's much more about keeping yourself connected to the Earth, the physical realms of the stars, and the universe around you and within you. If that means learning more about the universe, do it!

Getting what you need is a matter of seeing it and choosing it. Seeing what's within you, what's around you, and what your potential is are the keys to making a quantum leap to a better life!

Key Takeaways

- Quantum physics teaches us a lot about ourselves and the universe.

- Vibrational energy is a source of consciousness.

- Everyone has a unique relationship with the universe.

- The multiverse contains all possible universes, not just the one we know.

- Your brain, soul, or spirit helps you understand your place in the universe.

- Your potential helps you grow and develop into your future.

- What you need is already with you. Make that leap!

CONCLUSION

Congratulations! Now that you've finished reading *Push Your Limits*, you should have a game plan for improving your life. Primary among the concepts you've encountered is the power of connections.

What have you discovered within its pages? You've learned a lot about your body and your brain and how they work together. Rather than being two separate things, they're intimately connected. Together, they control multiple aspects of your life. Your thoughts and your emotions are both the result of the firing of neurons and synapses in the brain. Even your habits—the actions you perform without thinking—are carried out by your body in response to your brain. Your reactions to stimuli and your motivation couldn't exist without those connections.

Another theme you've explored is the patterns you live by. Your subconscious and conscious habits are controlled by a process in the brain that connects to your body and tells it what to do. Those habits can be good for your body, or they can cause problems. It's up to you what you choose. Even your subconscious habits can be controlled by the choices you make. Interrupting the cycle of habits is possible with practice.

In addition to your choices, your beliefs shape your thoughts and actions. They affect your world in significant ways. In a very real sense, your beliefs determine the world you live in and how you respond to it. But your beliefs can also throw up roadblocks that keep you from accomplishing what you want. Never fear! Now, you've learned the techniques to align your beliefs with your desires.

Also connected to your choices are your purpose in life and your goals. Discovering that purpose—your everyday purpose as well as your greater purpose—opens your spirit to letting your passions lead you into actions. Encountering your higher self provides inspiration that will be with you always as you travel your path to enlightenment.

Along the way, the motivation you've discovered will lead you to your goals. You will certainly encounter roadblocks along the way, but the confidence and resilience you've built will see you through. You're able to rise above obstacles and face failure as just another opportunity to find your way to success.

One of your most intimate connections is with yourself. Self-love and self-care are two aspects of this connection. Cultivating self-worth means that you believe you are worthy of love. It's the value you place on yourself. It enables you to form that inner connection with who you really are and your potential for success. Self-care is what allows you to reach that potential. Taking care of your own needs for bodily and mental health will empower you to make the most of your life. Seemingly simple actions can have the greatest effects on your well-being.

Perhaps the most profound connection you have is with the universe. Quantum physics reveals how you are part of the vast expanse of an infinite number of possible universes. It helps explain the vibrational energy that resonates within you, as well as within the smallest aspects of matter and the enormity of realms of existence you can only imagine. You are made of elements born in the very stars and share in their heritage. Even your spirituality has a basis in quantum theory and cosmic consciousness.

Most people look to the fields of science and technology for facts and an understanding of the way the physical world works. They consider spirituality or religion to nourish their souls and achieve transcendence. The universe itself addresses abstract concepts like high-frequency vibrations that encompass your oneness with the infinite. All these aspects of life are valuable and lead you to a sense of wholeness.

I would encourage you, if you haven't already done so, to try the exercises and techniques you'll find throughout the book. You can discover ways to boost your motivation by using the strength of your brain. Discover journaling and follow the prompts I've given—or develop your own inspirational topics. Foster healthy habits that will sustain you. Learn specific techniques like visualization and habit stacking that will lead you to transform bad habits into ones that will improve your life.

And that's not all! Other techniques you can try will help you develop affirmations that will boost your ability to succeed in life and conquer the doubts that block your progress. You'll learn how mindfulness and meditation can calm your spirit and leave you open to discovering your higher self. Ways to set goals that will see you through your life are presented. So are techniques that, paradoxically, allow you to transform rejection and failure into resilience and success. Specific self-care practices will help you build a stronger body, mind, and spirit.

Best of all, you'll have experienced the wonders of your connection with the stars and the universe. You'll learn to look within yourself and to the wonders of infinity to reveal your most basic needs as well as how you can achieve them.

All in all, through this book, you will have learned how to view yourself from the perspective of success. The power of pushing your limits will change your life!

I was born in London. Since I was young, I had dreams of becoming a famous athlete or a star musician. However, my imagination was grounded by family responsibilities. I had to interrupt my studies at age 16. My family moved to Italy, and after that, I had to work and study hard on a demanding educational path. It threw me immediately into a world of hurdles, both economic and social, as well as educational.

My continuous research, curiosity, and learning by doing have led to my successful career as a professional consultant in my field of business. Personal intuition has now led me to become a resource for many practitioners and young talents looking for guidance, both from a professional and human perspective.

www.ardyconstance.com

REFERENCES

8 tips to overcome failure. (n.d.). The LAB Miami. https://thelabmiami.com/8-tips-to-overcome-failure/

8 ways to identify your passions and purpose. (2015, June 10). Dowhatyouloveforlife. https://dowhatyouloveforlife.com/8-ways-to-identify-your-passions-and-purpose/

Aaron. (2023, March 8). *Self-care vs Self-love in Kintsugi Magazine Articles - Find your frequency.* Kintsugi. https://kintsugispace.com/self-care-vs-self-love/

Ackerman, C. (2018, July 20). *What is self-compassion and self-love? (Definition, quotes + books).* PositivePsychology.com. https://positivepsychology.com/self-compassion-self-love/

Adler Planetarium Staff. (2024, February 23). *The top three multiverse theories: Many worlds, bubble universes, and shadow matter.* Adler Planetarium. https://www.adlerplanetarium.org/blog/top-multiverse-theories-niyah-and-the-multiverse/

Alhanati, J. (2021, June 1). *Follow your passions, and success will follow.* Investopedia. https://www.investopedia.com/articles/pf/12/passion-success.asp

Andrew Cohen Quote. (n.d.). A-Z quotes. https://www.azquotes.com/quote/1319719?ref=higher-purpose

Anzaku, I. (2019, October 29). *What is a nerve? - Structure, function, types of nerves, nerve disorders.* BYJUS. https://byjus.com/biology/nerves/#:~:text=There%20are%20three%20types%20of

Athuraliya, A. (2019, September 26). *Goal setting process: 5 tried & tested steps with templates.* Creately Blog. https://creately.com/blog/project-management/goal-setting-process/

Babauta, L. (2009, November 11). *The short but powerful guide to finding your passion.* Zen Habits. https://zenhabits.net/the-short-but-powerful-guide-to-finding-your-passion/

Bhandari, T. (2023, April 19). *Mind-body connection is built into brain, study suggests*. Washington University School of Medicine in St. Louis. https://medicine.wustl.edu/news/mind-body-connection-is-built-into-brain-study-suggests/

Bhavani, R. (2023, July 10). *Unleash your limitless potential*. Medium. https://rishabh-bhavani.medium.com/unleash-your-limitless-potential-caf23c19d8bb

Bollinger, A. (2019, May 17). *How to improve self confidence for more successful goal setting*. Austin Bollinger. https://www.austinbollinger.com/blog/how-to-improve-self-confidence-for-more-successful-goal-setting/

Breines, J. (2015). *3 ways your beliefs can shape your reality*. Psychology Today. https://www.psychologytoday.com/us/blog/in-love-and-war/201508/3-ways-your-beliefs-can-shape-your-reality

Building your resilience. (2020, February 1). American Psychological Association. https://www.apa.org/topics/resilience/building-your-resilience

Caire, M. J., & Varacallo, M. (2018, November 13). *Physiology, synapse*. NIH.gov; StatPearls Publishing. https://www.ncbi.nlm.nih.gov/books/NBK526047/

Carl Sagan Quotes. (2019). Goodreads.com. https://www.goodreads.com/author/quotes/10538.Carl_Sagan

Ceruto, S. (2019, March 26). *Council post: The neuroscience of motivation: How our brains drive hard work and achievement*. Forbes. https://www.forbes.com/sites/forbescoachescouncil/2019/03/26/the-neuroscience-of-motivation-how-our-brains-drive-hard-work-and-achievement/?sh=2039adf45fcb

Chopra, D., & Kafatos, M. (2017, January 2). *Why you and the universe are one*. The Chopra Foundation. https://choprafoundation.org/consciousness/why-you-and-the-universe-are-one/

Clear, J. (2013). *Goal setting: A scientific guide to setting and achieving goals*. James Clear. https://jamesclear.com/goal-setting

Cooks-Campbell, A. (2022, May 26). *What self-love truly means and ways to cultivate it*. Betterup. https://www.betterup.com/blog/self-love

Cozma, I. (2023, October 23). *Values, passion, or purpose — Which should guide your career?* Harvard Business Review. https://hbr.org/2023/10/values-passion-or-purpose-which-should-guide-your-career

Cuncic, A. (2019). *What happens to your body when you're thinking?* Verywell
    Mind. https://www.verywellmind.com/what-happens-when-you-think-
    4688619

Davis, T. (2018, December 28). *Self-care: 12 ways to take better care of yourself.*
    Psychology Today. https://www.psychologytoday.com/us/blog/click-here-
    happiness/201812/self-care-12-ways-take-better-care-yourself

Deepak Chopra Quotes. (n.d.). BrainyQuote.
    https://www.brainyquote.com/quotes/deepak_chopra_599977

Denis Waitley Quotes. (n.d.). Goodreads.
    https://www.goodreads.com/author/quotes/5108.Denis_Waitley

deVries, L. (2023). *The ultimate guide to personal energy.* Lora Devries Intentional
    Living and Empowerment Expert.
    https://www.loradevries.com/blog/ultimate-guide-to-personal-energy

Duhigg, C. (2019). *Habits: How they form and how to break them.* Npr.org.
    https://www.npr.org/2012/03/05/147192599/habits-how-they-form-and-
    how-to-break-them

Edmondson, A. (2011, April). *Strategies for learning from failure.* Harvard
    Business Review. https://hbr.org/2011/04/strategies-for-learning-from-
    failure

Fahkry, T. (2021, September 22). *Why your reality is a mirror reflecting your
    inner world.* Linkedin. https://www.linkedin.com/pulse/why-your-
    reality-mirror-reflecting-inner-world-tony-fahkry/

Ferguson, N. (n.d.). *Self-care: 5 benefits + 10 easy to use ideas to practice.*
    Nicholasferguson. https://www.nicholasferguson.org/blog/self-care-5-
    benefits-10-easy-to-use-ideas-to-practice

Fernandez, E. (2022, November 22). *Brain experiment suggests that consciousness
    relies on quantum entanglement.* Big Think. https://bigthink.com/hard-
    science/brain-consciousness-quantum-entanglement/

Field, B. (2022, November 13). *7 ways to practice self-love.* Verywell Mind.
    https://www.verywellmind.com/ways-to-practice-self-love-5667417

Fight or flight response. (2022). Psychology Tools.
    https://www.psychologytools.com/resource/fight-or-flight-
    response/#:~:text=The%20fight%20or%20flight%20response

Fontenot, S. (2022, July 13). *Can vagus nerve stimulation help combat traumatic
    memories?* News Center. https://news.utdallas.edu/health-medicine/vns-
    fear-research-2022/

Glowiak, M. (2020, April 14). *What is self-care and why is it important for you?* Southern New Hampshire University. https://www.snhu.edu/about-us/newsroom/health/what-is-self-care

Goal setting guide: 7 steps to effective goal setting. (n.d.). Quantive. https://quantive.com/resources/articles/goal-setting

Gupta, S. (2022, September 30). *What is self-worth?* Verywell Mind. https://www.verywellmind.com/what-is-self-worth-6543764

Halber, D. (2018a, August 29). *Motivation: Why you do the things you do.* Brainfacts. https://www.brainfacts.org/thinking-sensing-and-behaving/learning-and-memory/2018/motivation-why-you-do-the-things-you-do-082818#:~:text=The%20regions%20of%20the%20brain

Halber, D. (2018b, September 6). *The anatomy of emotions.* Brainfacts. https://www.brainfacts.org/thinking-sensing-and-behaving/emotions-stress-and-anxiety/2018/the-anatomy-of-emotions-090618

Health Direct. (2018, March 9). *Motivation: How to get started and staying motivated.* Healthdirect Australia. https://www.healthdirect.gov.au/motivation-how-to-get-started-and-staying-motivated

How to be more resilient: 8 ways to build your resilience. (n.d.). Calm Blog. https://www.calm.com/blog/how-to-be-resilient

How to practice self-love. (n.d.). Headspace. https://www.headspace.com/mindfulness/self-love

How to set realistic goals. (n.d.). With You. https://www.wearewithyou.org.uk/advice-and-information/advice-for-you/how-to-set-realistic-goals#:~:text=A%20realistic%20goal%20is%20one

Indeed Editorial Team. (2023). *10 ways to boost your confidence in the workplace.* Indeed Career Guide. https://www.indeed.com/career-advice/career-development/ways-to-boost-your-confidence

Kirupa, L. (2024, February 2). *Signs you have a high vibration.* Her Campus. https://www.hercampus.com/school/york-u/signs-you-have-a-high-vibration/

Kozlowski, T. (2021, January 19). *How to assess our habits for growth.* Terri Kozlowski. https://terrikozlowski.com/habits-form-routines-for-success/#:~:text=Research%20from%20Duke%20University%20sites

Lent Hirsch, M. (2024, April 1). *Purpose: The definition and why it's good for you.* EverydayHealth. https://www.everydayhealth.com/emotional-health/all-about-having-a-sense-of-purpose-what-it-means-and-why-its-so-good-for-you/

Let go of your limiting beliefs with these 5 steps. (2019, July 7). Thehappinessdoctor. https://www.thehappinessdoctor.com/blog/let-go-of-your-limiting-beliefs-with-these-5-steps

MantraCare. (2022, March 25). *Behavior patterns | types | benefits | consequences | how to deal.* Therapy Mantra. https://therapymantra.co/self-care/behavior-patterns/#:~:text=There%20are%20four%20main%20types

Marschall, A. (2023, April 1). *How to deal with rejection.* Verywell Mind. https://www.verywellmind.com/how-to-deal-with-rejection-7260048

Martin, S. (2019, May 31). *What is self-love and why is it so important?* Psych Central. https://psychcentral.com/blog/imperfect/2019/05/what-is-self-love-and-why-is-it-so-important

Mayo Clinic Staff. (2020a, September 15). *Mindfulness exercises.* Mayo Clinic. https://www.mayoclinic.org/healthy-lifestyle/consumer-health/in-depth/mindfulness-exercises/art-20046356

Mayo Clinic Staff. (2020b, October 27). *How to build resiliency.* Mayo Clinic. https://www.mayoclinic.org/tests-procedures/resilience-training/in-depth/resilience/art-20046311

McLachlan, S. (2021, December 22). *The science of habit: How to rewire your brain.* Healthline. https://www.healthline.com/health/the-science-of-habit#14

Michaud, J. (n.d.). *Why is it important to explore your beliefs?* Jennifer Michaud & Associates. https://www.jennifermichaudassociates.com/blog-1/why-is-it-important-to-explore-your-beliefs

Michel, A. (2020, February 11). *The health benefits of loving yourself.* The Emily Program. https://emilyprogram.com/blog/the-health-benefits-of-loving-yourself/

Michio Kaku Quotes. (n.d.). Goodreads. https://www.goodreads.com/author/quotes/18800.Michio_Kaku

Mindfulness: What you need to know. (n.d.). McLean Hospital. https://www.mcleanhospital.org/essential/mindfulness#:~:text=Mindfulness%20training%20has%20been%20proven

Morin, A. (2019). *10 Healthy ways to bounce back from failure.* Verywell Mind. https://www.verywellmind.com/healthy-ways-to-cope-with-failure-4163968

Morin, A. (2024, January 26). *How to be more confident: 9 tips that work.* Verywell Mind. https://www.verywellmind.com/how-to-boost-your-self-confidence-4163098

Mosunic, C. (2023, November 2). *8 gratitude exercises to cultivate a more grateful mindset.* Calm Blog. https://www.calm.com/blog/gratitude-exercises

Mosunic, C. (n.d.). *The benefits of moving meditation and how to start practicing.* Calm Blog. https://www.calm.com/blog/moving-meditation

Moulder, H. (2021). *How to set goals for building self-confidence & fulfillment.* Course Correction Coaching. https://www.coursecorrectioncoaching.com/how-to-set-goals-for-building-self-confidence-and-fulfillment/

National Institute of Mental Health. (2022). *Caring for your mental health.* National Institute of Mental Health. https://www.nimh.nih.gov/health/topics/caring-for-your-mental-health

National Society of Leadership and Success. (n.d.). *Goal setting techniques: Ways to effectively set and achieve goals.* NSLS. https://www.nsls.org/goal-setting-techniques

Nowak, P. (2023, February 14). *Does your brain have a memory limit? (Explained!).* Www.linkedin.com. https://www.linkedin.com/pulse/does-your-brain-have-memory-limit-explained-paul-nowak/

Parasympathetic nervous system (PSNS): What it is & function. (2022b, June 6). Cleveland Clinic. https://my.clevelandclinic.org/health/body/23266-parasympathetic-nervous-system-psns

Parasympathetic nervous system (PSNS): What it is & function. (2022b, June 6). Cleveland Clinic. https://my.clevelandclinic.org/health/body/23266-parasympathetic-nervous-system-psns

Parker-Pope, T. (2017, July 25). *How to build resilience in midlife.* The New York Times. https://www.nytimes.com/2017/07/25/well/mind/how-to-boost-resilience-in-midlife.html

Paturel, A. (2024, March 21). *Bolster your brain by stimulating the vagus nerve.* Cedars-Sinai. https://www.cedars-sinai.org/blog/stimulating-the-vagus-nerve.html

Perry, E. (2022a, April 19). *Mindfulness vs meditation: How both can benefit you.* Betterup. https://www.betterup.com/blog/mindfulness-vs-meditation#:~:text=Mindfulness%20is%20a%20quality%20that

Perry, E. (2022b, August 3). *How to set realistic goals: 11 tips to reach the clouds with your feet on the ground*. Betterup. https://www.betterup.com/blog/how-to-set-realistic-goals

Perry, E. (2022c, December 19). *How to deal with rejection: 7 Tips*. BetterUp. https://www.betterup.com/blog/how-to-deal-with-rejection

Ponte, D., & Schäfer, L. (2013). Carl Gustav Jung, Quantum Physics and the Spiritual Mind: A Mystical Vision of the Twenty-First Century. *Behavioral Sciences, 3*(4), 601–618. https://doi.org/10.3390/bs3040601

Psychology Today. (2019). *Habit formation*. Psychology Today. https://www.psychologytoday.com/us/basics/habit-formation

Psychology Today. https://www.psychologytoday.com/us/blog/living-forward/202304/how-your-thinking-affects-your-brain-chemistry#:~:text=Thinking%20and%20brain%20chemistry%20is

QuoteFancy. (n.d.). *Ralph Marston Quote: "Your goals, minus your doubts, equal your reality."* Quotefancy.com. https://quotefancy.com/quote/1547749/Ralph-Marston-Your-goals-minus-your-doubts-equal-your-reality

Ratsamee, D. (2022, April 18). *Bring nature into your mindfulness practice with forest bathing*. The Whole U. https://thewholeu.uw.edu/2022/04/18/bring-nature-into-your-mindfulness-practice-with-forest-bathing/

Robbins, T. (n.d.). *12 tips on finding your purpose in life*. Tonyrobbins. https://www.tonyrobbins.com/stories/date-with-destiny/what-is-my-purpose/

Ruwa, R. (2023, February 11). *The 13 benefits of practising self-love*. Meer. https://www.meer.com/en/71075-the-13-benefits-of-practising-self-love

Seladi-Schulman, J. (2018, July 23). *What part of the brain controls emotions?* Healthline Media. https://www.healthline.com/health/what-part-of-the-brain-controls-emotions#the-limbic-system

Seppala, E. (2014, May 9). *The scientific benefits of self-compassion*. The Center for Compassion and Altruism Research and Education. https://ccare.stanford.edu/uncategorized/the-scientific-benefits-of-self-compassion-infographic/

Seppala, E. (2016). *3 powerful science-based benefits of a little self-love*. Psychology Today. https://www.psychologytoday.com/us/blog/feeling-it/201211/3-powerful-science-based-benefits-little-self-love

Shackman, A. J., & Wager, T. D. (2019). The emotional brain: Fundamental questions and strategies for future research. *Neuroscience Letters, 693,* 68–74. https://doi.org/10.1016/j.neulet.2018.10.012

Smithyman, T. (2023, May 31). *How to handle rejection.* Psyche. https://psyche.co/guides/how-to-handle-rejection-so-that-you-can-heal-and-move-on

Sofra, T. (2022, August 16). *The top 10 self-limiting beliefs and how to let them go.* Medium. https://medium.com/@traceysofra/the-top-10-self-limiting-beliefs-and-how-to-let-them-go-e94662a56f17

Stanborough, R. J. (2019, February 13). *Everything you need is inside you.* Healthline. https://unmistakablecreative.com/everything-youre-searching-is-within-you/

Stanborough, R. J. (2020, November 13). *What is vibrational energy? Definition, benefits & more.* Healthline. https://www.healthline.com/health/vibrational-energy

Stephen R. Covey Quote: "We are what we repeatedly do. Excellence, then, is not an act, but a habit. (n.d.). QuoteFancy. https://quotefancy.com/quote/1839842/Stephen-R-Covey-We-are-what-we-repeatedly-do-Excellence-then-is-not-an-act-but-a-habit

Stiles, J. (2011). Brain development and the nature versus nurture debate. *Progress in Brain Research, 189,* 3–22. https://doi.org/10.1016/b978-0-444-53884-0.00015-4

Strankowski, D. (n.d.). *Develop passion and desire for achieving your goals!* Ascend Careers. https://www.ascendcareers.net/project/develop-passion-and-desire-for-achieving-your-goals

Strong, R. (2022, September 19). *Your habits matter more than you might think — Here's why.* Healthline. https://www.healthline.com/health/mental-health/why-are-habits-important#types

Suttie, J. (2020, August 6). *Seven ways to find your purpose in life.* Greater Good. https://greatergood.berkeley.edu/article/item/seven_ways_to_find_your_purpose_in_life

7 neurotransmitters involved in the brain-body connection. (2020, April 3). Ask the Scientists. https://askthescientists.com/neurotransmitters/

Tanaaz. (2016, June 21). *Your inner vs. higher purpose.* Forever Conscious. https://foreverconscious.com/inner-vs-higher-purpose#google_vignette

Taylor, M. (2022, April 28). *What does fight, flight, freeze, fawn mean?* WebMD. https://www.webmd.com/mental-health/what-does-fight-flight-freeze-fawn-mean

Thackera, R. (2021, January 25). *Five truths about self-love: The benefits and how-tos.* Denver Metro Counseling. https://denvermetrocounseling.com/five-truths-about-self-love-the-benefits-and-how-tos/

10 ways to build confidence and work towards success. (2019, February 6). American Intercontinental University. https://www.aiuniv.edu/blog/2019/january/10-ways-build-confidence-success

25 self-worth and self-esteem quotes you needed to hear today. (n.d.). Verywell Mind. https://www.verywellmind.com/self-worth-and-self-esteem-quotes-8657014

Vagus nerve: Gastroparesis, vagus nerve stimulation & syncope.

Vagus nerve: Gastroparesis, vagus nerve stimulation & syncope. (2022a, January 11). Cleveland Clinic. https://my.clevelandclinic.org/health/body/22279-vagus-nerve

van Mulukom, V. (2023, February 20). *How your brain decides what to think.* The Conversation. https://theconversation.com/how-your-brain-decides-what-to-think-198109

Vilhauer, J. (2023, April 10). *How your thinking affects your brain chemistry.*

Wisner, W. (2024, June 21). *25 positive mental health affirmations to recite daily.* Verywell Mind. https://www.verywellmind.com/positive-daily-affirmations-7097067

Zhi, G., & Xiu, R. (2023). Quantum Theory of Consciousness. *Journal of Applied Mathematics and Physics, 11*(09), 2652–2670. https://doi.org/10.4236/jamp.2023.119174